ADVANCE PRAISE FOR DISASTER PROOF

"In today's volatile world, taking a wait-and-see approach will lead to disaster. Scenario planning is a way to make the future manageable."

MARK POWESKA, President & CEO, Hydro One

"Lance Mortlock provides a thorough and comprehensive knowledge base to position organizations for success under any conditions."

DR. JIM DEWALD, Dean of The Haskayne School of Business & Professor of Strategy & Entrepreneurship

"COVID-19 will reshape global economies forever. This book helps all leaders prepare for that future."

TIM PENKETH, Founder & CEO, TheFutureEconomy.ca

"The future is always uncertain and full of external risk; *Disaster Proof* offers a way to minimize that risk."

MARY MORAN, CEO, Calgary Economic Development

"This thought-provoking book offers a strategic tool to leaders and organizations who strive to deliver exceptional focus and execution during unpredictable and dynamic times."

MURRAY BICKLEY, President & CEO, Sanjel Energy Services

"*Disaster Proof* lays the foundation for any organization looking to build resilience in a complex world. The author makes envisioning, formulating, and executing scenarios an intuitive and — dare I say — fun process."

BOB SARTOR, President & CEO, Calgary Airport Authority

"Challenges my preconceived one-dimensional notions of the future. It addresses the critical issue of preparing and leading an organization to be nimble and responsive by imagining potential outcomes from multiple external risk factors."

ROBERT MORGAN, President & CEO, Strathcona Resources Ltd

"This essential guidebook reminds us that strategic management is the job of many in an organization but requires courageous thought leadership and a practical approach. *Disaster Proof* gives you tools to effect strategic change toward building a more resilient organization."

HELEN WELSEY, Chief Operating Officer, TECO Peoples Gas

"A strategic planners must-read. Introducing AI to the strategic planning process addressed in this book is game-changing and deserves serious consideration."

DARREN YAWORSKY, Chief Financial Officer, Badger Daylighting

"This book is a tremendous resource that provides a comprehensive understanding of this management practice and practical examples from experienced leaders. It helped me crystalize my thinking on how I will commit to this discipline going forward"

STEVE PHILLIPS, Executive Vice President, The Co-operators Group

"Provides business leaders with a pragmatic and powerful set of tools to navigate uncertainty and build organizational resilience by developing a critical organizational muscle: digitally-enabled agile scenario planning. An essential read for tomorrows leaders!"

PAUL SELWAY, Chief Digital Officer, AltaGas

"Lance Mortlock provides valuable lessons on business strategy at the most challenging time in the last 80 years."

RICHARD HASKAYNE, OC AOE, Canadian Businessman & Philanthropist

LANCE MORTLOCK

DISASTER PROOF

SCENARIO PLANNING
FOR A POST-PANDEMIC FUTURE

AI: THE NEW FRONTIER

BARLOW BOOKS
fine books for enterprising authors

Library and Archives Canada Cataloguing in Publication data available upon request.

978-1-988025-61-2 (hardcover)

Printed in Canada

Publisher: Sarah Scott
Book producer: Tracy Bordian/At Large Editorial Services
Cover design: Paul Hodgson
Interior design and layout: Ruth Dwight
Copy editing: Wendy Thomas
Proofreading: Eleanor Gasparik
Indexing: Karen Hunter

For more information, visit **www.barlowbooks.com**

Barlow Book Publishing Inc.
96 Elm Avenue, Toronto, ON
Canada M4W 1P2

BARLOW BOOKS

For my wife, Elisabeth

CONTENTS

INTRODUCTION

> *"There are three essential starting points for corporate strategy: global scenarios, competitive positioning and strategic vision. The first represents the world of possibility, the second the world of relativity and the third the world of creativity."*
>
> —PIERRE WACK (EXECUTIVE AT SHELL WHO FIRST DEVELOPED SCENARIO PLANNING IN THE PRIVATE SECTOR)

It's hard to imagine a bigger upheaval to the world as we've known it than the COVID-19 coronavirus pandemic. It's not just a global public health emergency; the turbulence arising from the disease hits businesses, governments, consumers, and, as a humanitarian crisis, society at large. The World Bank's 2020 Global Economic Prospects report predicts a 5.2 percent contraction in global GDP, the worst global recession in decades. Advanced economies are expected to shrink by 7 percent. On a human scale, anyone who has shifted from a workplace to a home office, especially if they're also dealing with children, is well aware of just one of the myriad effects of COVID-19. What makes it more frightening is that, as of this writing, no one knows how long it will last, what its long-term consequences will be, nor what the so-called new normal will look like.

The virus originated in Wuhan, China, where the first lockdown occurred in January 2020, and spread globally from there. It's tempting to say a medical catastrophe as sudden and unanticipated as this could not have been foreseen by anyone, but that's only partly true.

In October 2019, two months before the first recorded case of COVID-19 in Wuhan, the Washington-based Center for Strategic and International Studies (CSIS) decided to study the impact of a global health pandemic. Samuel Brannen, head of the Risk and Foresight Group at CSIS, and Kathleen Hicks, senior vice-president of CSIS, had in the past advised government officials, CEOs, and other leaders on how to plan for unforeseen crises. For this planning exercise, they chose three scenarios: the use of artificial intelligence by the Chinese military; a major cyberattack and disinformation campaign aimed at the United States; and, after consulting with scientists, a fictional novel and highly transmissible coronavirus similar to SARS and MERS, two other coronaviruses responsible for outbreaks in 2003–04 and 2012 respectively.

For the health crisis, Brannen and Hicks gathered a team of experts drawn from the fields of bioscience, global health, national security, emergency response, and economics to stress-test the ability of the United States to respond to a global health catastrophe. The parallels to what actually unfolded were striking. Their scenario projected a 3.125 percent death rate. (As of August 2020, the World Health Organization announced that about 3.4 percent of reported COVID-19 cases had died.) Their scenario assumed governments would try short-term measures to slow the spread, such as travel bans and border closures, which would not be successful. In fact, these moves would create mistrust and impede the international cooperation so necessary to combat a pandemic. Like COVID-19, the fictional virus in their scenario spread through international air travel, and those infected by the virus showed no symptoms for a period of time, increasing the likelihood of human-to-human transmission. The experts working on the scenario model could see enormous economic and political problems and overloaded health care systems, as well. Furthermore, the scenario assumed countries would use fiscal and monetary stimulus to prop up economies.[1]

The insights that came out of Brannen and Hicks's fictional, but surprisingly real, scenario exercise could have changed how the United States responded to COVID-19. One was the significance of early preventive measures. "Establishing trust and cooperation domestically and internationally among governments, companies, workers, and citizens is important before the crisis strikes," wrote Brannen and Hicks. And since viruses aren't stopped by borders, clear communication and information-sharing among nations was essential. But none of this happened. The fragile state of public trust in governments and leaders—the hyperpartisanship in the United States, for example, as well as various international tensions—made that almost impossible to achieve. Misinformation, deliberately spread by both mysterious foreign sources and elected officials alike, created suspicion and confusion. The exercise also emphasized the vital role of the private sector, the source of most of the technological innovation that could produce treatments or a cure. That was the one bright spot, as governments did reach out to create public–private partnerships in search of a vaccine.

If there was one overriding conclusion, it was that leaders don't take health issues seriously enough as a national security issue, and mistrust in NGOs dedicated to international coordination, such as the World Health Organization, means individual countries focus on domestic priorities with too little commitment to international coordination and collaboration. "Scenarios and foresight can be powerful tools to imagine a possible future," write Brannen and Hicks. "But we must do better. We must make policy that prevents and, where needed, prepares for those futures we do not want."[2]

■ ■ ■

Brannen and Hicks's scenario planning exercise proved how effective the practice can potentially be when used by public or private organizations. Had the U.S. government been able, and willing, to follow its recommendations, it could have avoided much of the chaos and distress that has unfolded.

Yet that is rarely how leaders decide. Whenever leaders of organizations make decisions, they make them in an environment of complexity and uncertainty. They study available data, make educated guesses, follow their gut instincts, but ultimately no one can see into the future. However, scenario planning can help leaders make the best, most informed choices.

In a sense, scenario planning is like chess. Although chess players cannot predict exactly what an opponent will do, skilled ones are able to visualize a number of potential moves ahead and develop strategies to deal with each one. Scenario planning teams identify potential developments that may happen in the future and create effective responses to them. Each scenario is a "snapshot" of the future—a disruptor emerges in an organization's sector; oil prices plummet; the firm loses its biggest client; the world is struck by a global pandemic. Planners can then evaluate the potential threats (and opportunities) and have on hand a response, if or when it's needed.

This book is essential reading for business leaders who want to prepare for future disasters because scenario planning is *the* invaluable tool for the 21st century, one that will help them navigate complex challenges and prepare creative responses for even the most perilous hazards.

In the pages that follow, I give you an in-depth guide to scenario planning. In Chapter 1, I take you through the evolution of scenario planning and how it fits into an organization's overall strategic plans and how it will improve performance. Then, in Chapter 2, I explore the two defining challenges of modern business—uncertainty and complexity. I show how scenario planning will help you develop responses to these challenges and build your organization's resilience. Chapter 3 is a step-by-step guide to building a scenario planning system for your organization. In Chapter 4, I explore the different levels at which scenario planning operates, from the macro, industry, and organizational level to that of individual employees. In Chapter 5, I walk you through the eight main benefits of scenario planning; Chapter 6 delves into the role played by scenario planners within your organization, working closely with the two most important leaders—the CEO and CSO. Chapter 7 is devoted to the new frontier of scenario planning, integrating it with artificial intelligence and big data to superpower your organization's capabilities. And, in the concluding Chapter 8, I sum up the value of scenario planning to every organization and the role it will play in the increasingly complex and volatile future.

How did I come to scenario planning? There wasn't a single "Aha!" moment, but over time I tested the approach with many clients on different projects and the results were consistently successful.

I've spent my career helping clients in Asia, the Middle East, Europe, and North and South America solve very complex problems, gradually moving into scenario planning as I realized how effective it was. As a strategic advisor, you're always looking for new ideas and tools to help leaders and organizations succeed, grow, and adapt. But I'm also a high achiever, always striving to be the best I can be at my craft, ensuring I'm on top of the latest thinking and research so I can respond to my clients' toughest questions with thoughtful and insightful answers.

After completing a science degree at the University of Exeter, I did an MBA at Cardiff Business School at Cardiff University in Wales in 1999 and 2000. Although scenario planning as a concept had been around for some time, it was only briefly introduced and discussed during my studies, not given the kind of attention I now think it deserves. At the time, the flavours of the day were "lean manufacturing," a method of production originally pioneered at Toyota in the 1930s and updated for the 90s, and "Six Sigma," the technique developed by Motorola and famously applied to General Electric in the mid-90s by then-CEO Jack Welch. What they had in common was a focus on operational, not long-range strategic, processes.

As I moved into the workforce, I spent 10 years at Accenture plc and the past decade at Ernst & Young LLP, both global giants in the consulting and professional services space. During this period, I've been involved in more than 150 consulting projects for more than 60 organizations in 11 countries.

Throughout my career I've never stopped pursuing further studies. I was part of Harvard Business School's High Potential Leadership program in 2010, and in 2015, I was among the first cohort of a year-long corporate innovation program at Stanford University's Graduate School of Business. I acquired strategic business tools and techniques to accelerate change within organizations. Three years later, I completed an executive program called Artificial Intelligence and Implications for Business Strategy run by MIT's Sloan School of Management and the Computer Science and Artificial Intelligence Laboratory (CSAIL). Focusing on key AI technologies such as machine learning, natural language processing, and robotics, I learned how these new technologies apply to organizational strategies and came to understand the economic and societal issues they raise.

These and other programs I've taken over the years have given me the kind of sophisticated background to help clients adjust to the enormously challenging 21st century.

My earliest exposure to scenario planning was with the global oil and gas company Shell in Europe in 2003 and 2004 while I was living and working in Aberdeen, Scotland. Its upstream division managed the exploration and extraction of crude oil and natural gas in the North Sea, and I worked on a project with the Upstream Corporate Planning group to help coordinate the complex planning and analysis required to implement a major new IT system. I was also involved in improving Shell's practices regarding business planning and on knowledge and best practice, sharing sessions between Shell and RWE AG, a big German electrical utilities company. At the time, I was less than five years into my career and was getting a very important education even if I didn't appreciate at the time the extent to which Shell had evolved scenario planning, essentially writing the playbook that others would follow.

Despite hearing about scenario planning at Shell, I was still mastering simple strategy development and strategic planning concepts and their applications when I came to Canada in 2008. A lot of the work I was initially doing with clients involved developing "static" strategies. I would help them articulate strategic objectives and focus business plans but spent little time thinking through how the strategies would evolve and adapt based on how different external scenarios might play out. While the most progressive global organizations, like Shell, Anglo American plc, UPS, and others, were invested in scenario planning, in my experience, whether it was oil and gas, mining, power and utilities, manufacturing, or the public sector, few clients were asking scenario-type questions of their consultants or their internal planning teams.

Gradually I realized that leaders needed to take scenario planning more seriously, particularly given the increasing level of global uncertainty and complexity. The strategies adopted by organizations I was working with were not agile enough to adapt to our increasingly unpredictable and erratic world. I understood that for strategic plans to be more dynamic and flexible, the solution was scenario planning.

Starting in 2015, I was regularly applying and integrating scenario planning into most strategy projects, because the benefits were unambiguous. When I developed strategies with a management team, the companies' boards were engaged and pleased with what management presented to them. I've always believed that the best strategic advisor combines both academic and practical knowledge and skills, so most recently, my research at the University of Calgary's Haskayne School of Business centres on scenario planning, including the application of AI.

What will scenario planning do for you?

Scenario planning has already proven its value in many applications. Now, as we work our way through, and eventually out of, the COVID-19 pandemic, I believe we'll see scenario planning emerge as the indispensable tool that it is, one that, much like the chess analogy, helps managers evaluate the dynamics of the competitive environment and potential future developments, and set up goals and long-range plans for success. This is my guide to walk you through it.

CHAPTER 1

WHAT IS SCENARIO PLANNING?

"Imagination is everything. It is the preview of life's coming attractions."

—ALBERT EINSTEIN

In October 2018, the Johns Hopkins Center for Health Security, the World Economic Forum, and the Bill & Melinda Gates Foundation co-hosted Event 201, a macro-level scenario planning exercise that simulated an outbreak of a novel coronavirus transmitted from bats to pigs (in Brazilian farms) to human beings, leading to a world pandemic. It was modelled after the SARS outbreak of 2003–04, but a more transmissible version involving even people with mild symptoms.

When I looked at the results of this fictional scenario, I was struck by two things. First, it's uncanny how accurately this group "imagined the future," fully two months before the first known case of COVID-19 occurred in Wuhan, China, and three months before the first confirmed case in the United States. Secondly, Event 201 was a model example of how an effective scenario planning works and what it can do for businesses as well as the public sector.[1]

It did everything right. It involved a range of stakeholders—in this case from academe, business, government, and the health sector. The discussions took place in workshop-style formats. And the planners had created a carefully crafted narrative for the scenario. Once the epidemic became established, it exploded into a global pandemic mainly because no one listened to the experts who were issuing warnings. At first, some countries seemed to control it, but eventually the virus continued its spread. There was no vaccine available in the first year. There were major societal and economic consequences, and a conviction that the worst of it could have been avoided in the early going had there been the political will. (Does this sound familiar?)

The recommendations were the following:

- Global cooperation is essential.
- Major gaps in preparedness (for example, a global shortage of masks) need to be addressed.
- Corporate capabilities need to be used since the public sector will soon be overwhelmed (for example, Dyson Ltd.'s ability to create ventilators).
- Nations, international organizations, and global transportation companies should cooperate to ensure trade and travel can continue during a severe pandemic.
- Governments should provide more resources and support for the surge manufacturing of vaccines, therapeutics, and diagnostics so badly needed in a pandemic.
- Businesses need to recognize the economic burden of pandemics and lobby for stronger preparedness.
- Governments and the private sector should assign a greater priority to combating misinformation and disinformation.

■ ■ ■

Scenario planning originated with the military and has been firmly rooted in military strategy, usually in the form of "war games," throughout history, noted Ron Bradfield and a team from the business school at Glasgow's University of Strathclyde in their 2005 paper, "The Origins and Evolution of Scenario Techniques in Long Range Business Planning."[2] Furthermore, they note, in the late 1950s Herman Kahn developed scenarios at the RAND Corporation to create different strategies for dealing with the Soviet Union during the Cold War. More recently, as Michael Fitzsimmons has written in his 2019 book, *Scenario Planning and Strategy in the Pentagon,* the U.S. Department of Defense has used a formalized scenario planning process to support strategy and force development since 2002.

Over the last several decades, techniques in scenario planning have evolved, with considerable research done on its application within large organizations. Among the most important were Shell's Year 2000 study initiated in 1967 and General Electric's early experiments with scenario planning around the same time. Many studies since then have provided evidence that the tool has an impact on performance.

But for almost 50 years, the global oil and gas giant Shell has been the leader in developing scenarios to understand possible futures and deepen the company's strategic thinking. It has helped numerous management teams explore ways to chart a path forward and make more informed decisions, and as a result, it has usually been ahead of its competitors. Shell's scenario planning challenged assumptions and considered a range of potential developments, always encouraging its leaders to stretch their thinking and mental models beyond the typical comfort zone. (Mental models are those beliefs or visions we carry in our minds about how a concept or framework will work.) The company's scenarios also inform the thinking of governments, businesses at large, and academia in transformative ways.[3]

In this chapter we explore the definition of scenario planning and how it evolved over the decades from its early use in military planning to its application at Shell a few decades later. To set the appropriate context, a couple of models illustrate how scenario planning integrates with a larger strategic management process and its main purpose in driving organizational performance.

SCENARIO PLANNING DEFINED

The time management expert Alan Lakein once said that "planning is bringing the future into the present so that you can do something about it now."[4] Scenario planning takes that much further. It is about making informed assumptions on what the future is going to bring and how the environment within which an organization operates will change over time. It is about identifying potential uncertainties or opportunities that an organization may face and challenging prevailing assumptions.

As the University of Strathclyde's Ron Bradfield explained, scenario planning involves many different words, such as *thinking, forecasting, analysis, learning, strategic flexibility, mental models, options,* and more. Strategic management consultant George Burt, in his 2003 paper, "First Steps: Towards Purposeful Activities in Scenario Thinking and Future Studies,"[5] suggests that scenario planning is the ability to learn faster than your competitors, and it may be the only source of true competitive advantage today. So scenarios are tools to research our understanding of the external world, to understand its dynamics in a more purposeful way, and to be prepared to think through the possible realities that might play out.

Scenario planning is like a playbook. It provides different chapters that represent different options—both favourable and unfavourable—for an organization to consider, enabling leaders to examine the downside, or worst-case, scenario, as well as the upside, or best-case, scenario. For another way of looking at it, Dan Collins, director of strategy at Suncor Energy, a Canadian oil and gas company, once said to me that scenario planning is about "stress testing and validating the strategy against multiple future plausible realities. It provides a tool that stretches perspectives, encourages stakeholders to collaborate, and tests the resilience of a company against those alternative futures."

Scenario planning offers a way to stretch mental models of organizations, enables greater organizational learning, and is found to inspire all kinds of questions from a strategic point of view that would otherwise not be asked. It prompts questions about the resiliency of an organization, revealing how well it can react and adapt when it encounters trouble (a topic covered in Chapter 2). It also questions whether management really understands how long their organization could survive under tough market conditions and whether it has levers at its disposal to react to external forces. Ultimately, scenario planning tests whether a strategy that is in place will work, needs to be adapted, or should be replaced.

In any organization there are typically gaps in understanding the external world and its uncertainties and threats. Scenario planning helps close those gaps by taking a very pragmatic approach to understanding those uncertainties and threats in a structured, methodical way. It also provides specific tools to deal with the complexity and uncertainty and can help with the potential gaps in understanding. Furthermore, scenarios provide a script-like *characterization* of possible futures presented in detail, with a special emphasis on casual connections and inter-consistency between different elements in the system.

Organizations are often stuck in a given moment, preoccupied with issues of the day, reacting to market changes, making decisions in real time, and failing to step back to truly understand the larger forces developing around them. Scenario planning enables organizations to pause rather than accelerate, slow things down to consider deeper and more strategic horizons so they're better equipped to speed things up later.

In summary, scenario planning is an imaginative exercise to articulate what the future could look like and identify ways to respond to it. It helps solve complex organizational problems through non-traditional thinking and decision-making.

SCENARIO PLANNING IN THE BROADER STRATEGY CONTEXT

According to Bain & Co.'s 2018 Management Tools and Trends report, topping the list of the 25 most popular management tools is strategic planning, which is the process of defining what a business should be and how best to achieve that outcome. It's also interesting that according to this global survey, the number of management tools being used today compared to a decade ago has fallen by half; tools generally don't work well when leaders use several of them on a limited basis as short-term fixes for fundamental problems.[6]

It's easy to get overwhelmed by the many different strategy-related activities and supporting tools, so it's important to understand how scenario planning fits within the broader context of strategy. Outlined below is a general overarching framework for strategy setting and strategic planning that illustrates the relationships and considerations that help set the context of where scenario planning fits between helping deal with market uncertainty and business complexity and driving a firm's performance.

This framework does not describe or propose anything groundbreaking but helps explain the different elements of importance when considering the application of scenario planning in a business context and how the different components fit together as part of strategy development.

Strategic planning is a highly structured and systematic exercise, usually dominated by an organization's leader, that establishes an overall mission as well as a vision for the future, followed by a series of steps to achieve that goal. It is, in many respects, two-dimensional. Scenario planning takes things into a three-dimensional future. By designing several possible, and plausible, scenarios—they might be positive or negative— scenario planning prepares an organization's leaders for unforeseen challenges, for some potential *what-ifs*. *What if* government introduces new regulations that constrain your organization? *What if* a conflict across the world disrupts your supply flow? *What if* a disruptor emerges in your sector and shakes up the status quo?

FIGURE 1
Strategy and Planning Layers Within an Organization

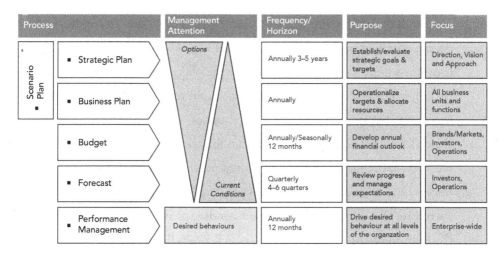

Process		Management Attention	Frequency/ Horizon	Purpose	Focus
Scenario Plan	Strategic Plan	Options	Annually 3–5 years	Establish/evaluate strategic goals & targets	Direction, Vision and Approach
	Business Plan		Annually	Operationalize targets & allocate resources	All business units and functions
	Budget		Annually/Seasonally 12 months	Develop annual financial outlook	Brands/Markets, Investors, Operations
	Forecast	Current Conditions	Quarterly 4–6 quarters	Review progress and manage expectations	Investors, Operations
	Performance Management	Desired behaviours	Annually 12 months	Drive desired behaviour at all levels of the organzation	Enterprise-wide

Market uncertainty and business complexity are the macro drivers to which organizations need to respond and react if they hope to maintain their performance goals. Smart organizations typically set a strategy (vision, mission, and objectives) and use scenario planning to validate and stress-test the strategy to ensure that nothing has been missed: gaps have been closed, resources allocated, all eventualities considered. The resulting flexibility then helps build a strategic plan for the year ahead. These different strategy-related components don't exist in a perfect sequence, but for simplicity have been represented this way and likely integrate with each other bi-directionally and in some cases in parallel before a strategic plan is set in motion and executed in the year ahead.

Scenario planning straddles the strategic planning and business planning processes, acting as a facilitator helping leadership teams consider broader options, evaluate strategies and plans, assess risks, and stress-test strategic initiatives. By presenting a number of potential options, scenario planning helps strategists evaluate different possibilities. It ensures that more than one option is seriously considered, and it forces strategists to think about what the organization would have to do in different scenarios.

As illustrated by the Management Attention column in Figure 1, the degree to which options are considered is high at the top of chart and becomes less important as you move down the planning layers. This illustrates the importance of scenario planning as a tool to support options analysis: it ensures that more than one strategic option is considered and identifies the different paths an organization can follow as measured against potential external realities. It also helps organizations consider how allocating resources to a new course of action would play out in each scenario. Furthermore, the importance of current conditions increases from the top to the bottom of the planning layers, which again illustrates the importance of the scenario planning role in envisioning future realities, not current conditions. It's about what *could be*, not what is.

It's also essential to consider how scenario planning informs performance management. For scenario planning to work there must be appropriate "signposts" established, which I describe in Chapter 3. Performance Management in Figure 1 shows key performance indicators (KPIs), both internal and external, that an organization uses to measure whether it is achieving its strategy. Call it "organizational health." There needs to be a strong alignment between what is measured from a scenario perspective—an early warning system allowing leaders to know whether a scenario is playing out or not—and the measurement of a firm's strategy. As the American author Seth Godin said, "If you measure it, it will improve." According to research firm Gartner, PepsiCo identifies the right performance indicators by mapping the information needed at key business decision points at different levels of the organization to reframe strategic questions and identify executive leaders' and operational KPIs.[7] (We discuss scenario planning levels further in Chapter 4.)

In summary, scenario planning does not exist in isolation, as the sole answer to strategy-related planning processes but is yet another weapon in the armoury of tools that can help inform a better strategy development process.

CASE STUDY
Manitoba Hydro (Enhancing Risk Management)

Manitoba Hydro is the electric power and natural gas utility in the province of Manitoba, Canada. Founded in 1961, it is a provincial Crown corporation, governed by the Manitoba Hydro-Electric

Board and the Manitoba Hydro Act. Today, the company operates 15 interconnected generating stations. It has more than 527,000 electric power customers and more than 263,000 natural gas customers.

WHY AND HOW SCENARIO PLANNING WAS USED

Manitoba Hydro defines scenario planning as the method by which its management envisions and plans for future eventualities. It answers the question, "If one of those scenarios were to come true, what would we do in the best interests of Manitobans?" Each scenario consists of different features or variables that describe the scenario from different perspectives, including, for example, social, technological, economic, political, and environmental factors. Furthermore, the different scenarios themselves are different collections of features or variables that come together in unique and distinctive ways. Manitoba Hydro uses scenario planning integrated with a long-term strategic plan and specifically uses it in resource planning of next-generation assets.

When Manitoba Hydro performs scenario planning, the management team asks a set of important questions as part of the process, including these:

- What are potential futures in the evolving energy landscape considering the three big trends of digitization, decarbonization, and decentralization?

- Considering the potential futures, what would it mean to the organization and Manitobans?

- What risks and uncertainties do they need to protect the company and Manitobans against and what kind of opportunities exist?

• What is the expected pace of change and underlying assumptions?

ORGANIZATIONAL BENEFITS AND RESULTS

For Manitoba Hydro the major benefits of scenario planning include *strategy validation and testing;* it helps the organization think in a different way and confirm that their plans make sense strategically and they've considered all possibilities. It also supports *enhanced risk management;* helping the organization be creative about imagining the future risks and ensuring the right preparations are in place.

In 2020, the emergence of the COVID-19 global pandemic forced Manitoba Hydro to consider scenario planning in the shorter term. The organization needed to pivot, developing and evaluating more real-time scenarios from a contagion perspective and understanding the impacts each one could have. Scenario planning is now considered a very powerful tool that can free up leaders to think differently and stretch mental models in a post COVID-19 world.[8]

SCENARIO PLANNING THEORY AND EVOLUTION

Thomas Chermack explains the links between scenario planning, learning, mental models—defined as an individual's frame of reference used to analyze problems—and decisions that impact performance.[9] He describes how the theory of scenario planning is set in motion by generating scenarios that are relevant to the circumstances an organization faces. He outlines how scenarios *provoke dialogue,* test decisions, and improve performance. Scenarios alter *mental models* to help individuals see new insights and revisit old assumptions about the organization and its future positioning. When it's successful, scenario planning can inspire more diverse, more robust, and better-challenged options.

Scenario planning also helps take into account what is both predictable and uncertain. As Kees van der Heijden pointed out in his 2000 paper, "Scenarios and Forecasting: Two Perspectives," scenario planning looks for *causality* and helps explain why observed patterns happen and then tries to explain them. Scenarios are also tools to examine our understanding of the world, challenge assumptions about the future, and highlight different aspects of a situation, whereby new gaps in understanding become apparent.[10]

It's also fair to say that scenario planning comes in waves, with many different established techniques emerging, according to W. R. Huss and E. J. Honton's 1987 paper, "Scenario Planning—What Style Should You Use." These include intuitive logic, trend impact analysis, and cross-impact analysis.[11]

Scenarios give managers the ability to *re-perceive reality*, since relevant information often goes unnoticed because of entrenched attitudes or a resistance to the process. George Burt and Kees van der Heijden found that small-and medium-sized organizations struggle with the application of scenario planning because managers tend to get caught up in the day-to-day, getting fixated with current events, focused more internally on the transaction environment, and fail to focus on the broader external environment. In smaller organizations, the level and quality of strategic conversations was found to be less advanced, group think prevailed, and short termism resulted in a preference for shorter incremental performance times.[12]

Burt and van der Heijden proposed a theoretical model whereby organizations that speed up the perception of approaching new realities are found to make sense of new realities earlier, understand available information, engage in strategic conversations, create the mental space for more powerful strategies, articulate a range of options, and know how, and when, to act.

Scenario planning helps stakeholders understand their situation within their organization's system with more clarity, understanding, and awareness. Scenarios also support how the organization interacts within the system with regard to relationships and connection points that influence outcomes. Scenarios help drive strategic actions and shift decision-making toward what an organization needs to do to influence outcomes.

Finally, C. A. Varum and C. Melo, in their 2010 paper, "Directions in Scenario Planning Literature—A Review of the Past Decades," provide an excellent overall review of scenario planning, summarizing articles into what-it-is articles, why-use-it articles, and how-to articles, aspects of which have been adopted in this specific literature review for ease of understanding.[13]

IMPORTANCE OF DRIVING ORGANIZATIONAL PERFORMANCE

Strategy is important because it sets the future direction of the company and provides a blueprint to competitive advantage and, ultimately, a firm's performance. Scenario planning, a vital management tool to help with the overarching strategy process, is critical to driving improvements in performance.

Scenario planning affects an organization's performance by enabling innovation, changing culture and behaviours, promoting broader stakeholder involvement in the strategy development process, and supporting dynamic capabilities, defined as a firm's ability to reconfigure and integrate internal and external resources and competencies to react, adapt, and shape the organization in a rapidly changing market environment.

Scenario planning, as detailed in "The Tenuous Link Between Formal Strategic Planning and Financial Performance," a 1987 paper researched by a team led by John Pearce at Villanova University, enables experiential learning, enhanced mental models, and better decision-making.[14]

One interesting research study, published in 2001 by Robert Phelps and two colleagues at the University of Surrey's European Management School, looked at the application of scenario planning in both the water and IT consulting industries in the United Kingdom.[15] The study found that larger companies in the water industry that have more resources tended to do more scenario planning. In the IT consulting industry, organizations that used scenario planning reported enhanced decision-making and greater efficiencies as well as increased financial performance, but again overall firm performance was not impacted.

Despite limited research on the link between scenario planning and firm performance, scores of organizations are using this tool, and with the onset of the global pandemic, more will in the future. As Paul Schoemaker, of the Wharton School of Business, reported in a 1995 article, "Scenario Planning: A Tool for Strategic Thinking," Royal Dutch Shell, the early adopter of scenario planning, has been consistently better in its oil forecasts than other major oil companies and was the first to recognize the overcapacity in the tanker business and Europe's petrochemical industry.[16]

In summary, scenario planning is a tool developed to help organizations stress-test and validate strategies by considering a range of possible futures that can be both favourable and unfavourable. It informs strategic objectives and initiatives so that the organization can be ready as the market plays out.

■ ■ ■

SUMMARY KEY POINTS

- Scenario planning is the process of considering alternative and possible future realities that are plausible and understanding the potential impacts on an organization both good and bad.

- Scenario planning helps organizations manage and mitigate external uncertainties in the market and internal complexities within the business.

- Scenario planning forms part of the wider strategy development process and acts as a tool to stress-test strategies informing the strategic plan and business plan.

- Scenario planning is more about considering future options and less about current conditions.

- Performance management systems are influenced by scenario planning in that signposts can be key performance indicators that help organizations monitor what scenarios might be playing out in real time.

- The military used scenario planning several decades ago, and as a concept it was further developed by Shell in the 1970s and 1980s.

- Scenario planning has been found to positively impact organizational performance and results.

- Scenario planning helps organizations and its leaders think strategically.

CHAPTER 2

COMPLEXITY AND UNCERTAINTY EXPLAINED

"Fear, uncertainty and discomfort are your compasses toward growth. If you run you stand a chance of losing, but if you don't run you've already lost."

—BARACK OBAMA, 44TH PRESIDENT OF THE UNITED STATES

Devils Tower is an impressive butte in northeastern Wyoming, rising 1,267 feet above the Belle Fourche River. It was the first national monument in the United States, established in 1906 by former president Theodore Roosevelt, and 400,000 annual visitors come to see it and hike the more than 1,000 acres within its boundaries. It falls under the jurisdiction of the National Park Service (NPS), an agency of the United States Department of the Interior that has an annual budget of more than $2.9 billion and manages all national parks, many national monuments, and other conservation and historical properties.

NPS is engaged in forward-looking stewardship, which, in an era of continuous climate change, requires an effective approach to assessing the uncertainty of what could happen in the parks it supervises as the world continues to warm. NPS was interested in using scenario planning as a structured approach to work with external uncertainties and better understand potential climate change implications as it applied to Devils Tower National Monument.

There is nothing more complex or uncertain than climate change, which, other than artificial intelligence, poses perhaps the greatest threat to the human species. Climate change is causing the melting of glaciers, declining snowpack, rising sea levels, warming oceans, and more frequent droughts and flooding. NPS chose to use scenario planning as a "climate change adaptation" tool. Scenario planning is flexible enough to allow, in this case, a way to understand the implications of climate change that is relevant to both resource and landscape management.

The service began its scenario planning process with an orientation phase, in which members of the team were introduced to the park's resources and over seven weeks consulted park staff and other experts to characterize the sensitivity of various areas. They created four "climate futures"—named Spearfish, Still DETO, Blazin' Hot, and Western Kansas—and studied key factors, including temperature, precipitation, soil moisture, and summer water deficits, to outline the ways climate change could affect elements such as wildlife, vegetation, aquatic resources, and visitors.

The benefits of applying scenario planning included the following:

- Increased understanding of crucial uncertainties facing resource management
- Incorporation of alternative perspectives into resource management planning
- Improved capacity for adaptive management to achieve desired conditions

By applying scenarios to each resource in the system managed by NPS, the team was able to better consider what could be done to minimize the effects of climate change from a strategic perspective. Strategic conversations were recognized as a major outcome that the service felt helped its staff members better understand their jobs. Due to the scenario planning process, teams began to take note of certain parts of the park that were at high risk and found themselves able to quickly respond when it was necessary to do so. The team that initially conducted the scenario planning hosted workshops with other outside stakeholders in order to engage them in the process and, most importantly, seek help and technical guidance with issues.

The scenario planning process guided NPS's understanding of the park beyond simply resource management into visitor policy and facilities and operational management. All these business strategies and tactics became more flexible based on the external signals and signposts growing out of the scenario planning exercise.[1]

■ ■ ■

Perhaps one of the greatest tests that leaders face is creating certainty in the face of uncertainty, when employees are asking hard questions for which leaders don't necessarily have all the answers. Leadership in this world is tough and, at times, lonely, and charting a path forward in the face of adversity is challenging at the best of times. In this chapter we explore what complexity and uncertainty mean, how they affect leadership strategy, and why it is important to understand the external environment and techniques used to mitigate the impacts of that strategy. Furthermore, several simple concepts are made easy to understand; these include understanding external risks, and how, through business resilience, systems thinking, intelligent organizational capability, and strategic anticipation, leaders can do a better job of managing risks and better answering those tough employee questions.

It's not only about managing risk. Organizations must become better at understanding the external world, at understanding relationships between different trends and drivers in the world, and at building strategies that can stand the test of time. It's a call to action for leaders and here is a compelling reason why. A Credit Suisse note to investors in 2017 reported that the average age of an S&P 500 company has dropped from 60 years in the 1950s to under 20 years today. The Wall Street firm says the trend is accelerating and one of the main drivers is disruption from technology.[2]

COMPLEXITY AND UNCERTAINTY DEFINED

The common definition of complexity, according to the *Collins Advanced English Dictionary*, is "the state of having many different parts connected or related to each other in a complicated way." For our purposes, I prefer "a measure of the total number of properties transmitted by an object and detected by an observer." Such a collection of properties is often referred to as a "state," which is intricate and complicated. In physical systems, complexity is a measure of the probability of the state vector of the system. Typically, as organizations grow in size and types of services and products, the level of complexity increases. For example, with increased size, the ability to manage individuals, teams of people, and departments requires enhanced governance and decision-making tools. Business processes are implemented to help standardize how work gets done; layers in the organizational structure are instituted; new technology systems are implemented; and different reporting mechanisms, including key performance metrics, are created to manage, control, and report on activities.

Uncertainty also produces doubt. When the economy is going bad and everyone is concerned about what will happen next, it can create apprehension and confusion. Risk taking, which requires a certain fearlessness and audacity, is another action affected by uncertainty, because outcomes are always hard to predict and measure.

Furthermore, the level of uncertainty changes all the time; can vary by sector, country, and region; and can accelerate at a different pace in different market contexts. For example, in the oil and gas sector, uncertainty is increasing with the move to more green economies, social licence issues, climate change challenges, and public awareness.

The questions that most business leaders constantly ask themselves is whether they are ready to survive or thrive in a world of accelerating complexity and uncertainty. The second question is how to react and adapt in a way that keeps employees productive and businesses profitable in the prevailing market environment.

A "black swan," a term coined by Nassim Nicholas Taleb in his 2007 book, *The Black Swan: The Impact of the Highly Improbable,* is defined as a rare, severe, and unforeseen event. A "double black swan" is even more rare, severe, and unforeseen. So, in the context of the oil and gas industry in the medium term, for example, there is considerable uncertainly, representing a double black swan event, due in part to a crash in global oil prices caused by Russia and Saudi Arabia flooding the market with crude oil, thus increasing supply, but also to a slowdown in demand from large economies like China and India caused by COVID-19. In the longer term, there are also more fundamental complexities and uncertainties at play. These include the following:

- A change in consumer demand with the emergence of electric vehicles
- The limited availability of capable talent wanting to join the industry
- Waning shareholder confidence symbolized by organizations like BlackRock and HSBC proactively moving away from the sector

- External stakeholders like OPEC controlling crude oil prices with limited ability of non-OPEC countries to change or influence
- An aging infrastructure
- The broader social licence to operate, caused by changing societal norms (climate and economic changes, global conflicts, health threats) becoming more challenging to navigate

Other sectors, including communications and high tech, have also experienced a huge amount of uncertainty over the past few years, in part due to the effort to stay at the forefront of constantly evolving technologies, like 5G and wireless, but also due to changing consumer behaviours and more sophisticated wants and needs through the application of user-centred design. In the pharmaceutical sector, when new drugs and vaccines are being developed, managing the product lifecycle from ideation to commercialization is fraught with risk and uncertainty, with no guaranteed payout at the end. According to *Biopharmaceutical Research & Development (PhRMA)*, on average it takes about 10 years for a new medicine to be developed from initial idea, to clinical trials, to commercialization, and each drug can cost an estimated $2.6 billion.[3]

Since early 2020, in the aerospace sector, we've seen uncertainty play out in real time with the impact of COVID-19—in some cases passenger traffic has been reduced by more than 90 percent at some airports, which is beyond even the most dire predictions. According to the Bureau of Transportation Statistics, which measures 24 airlines that carry 99 percent of passengers in the United States, in April 2020 the industry recorded a 96 percent reduction in airline passengers when compared to 2019.[4] Furthermore, recent crashes of Boeing's new Max 8, blamed on flight control problems as well as signs of angle-of-attack (AoA) sensor and instrument failures, created specific risks and uncertainties for Boeing that could not have been predicted.

These business complexities and uncertainties raise some important questions for leadership teams in the future, including the following:

- How will the global competitive environment evolve in the future?
- How can we effectively manage the direction of the portfolio?
- Is the strategy weatherproof?
- What will the industry look like in the future?
- Are we prepared to effectively manage the risks to which the company is exposed?
- Have all possible strategic options been considered?
- How can we monitor the changing environment?
- Is a global recession coming?
- How long will it take to recover from COVID-19?
- What type of government can we expect in the future?
- What technologies should we be worried about?

But perhaps the most important question is identifying what is simply "noise in the system," versus what an organization really needs to worry about at the time. With the staggering volume of information being generated from all kinds of sources, it becomes difficult to know what to pay attention to and what to ignore, compounded by the limitation of resource capacity to monitor and process all this information. The answers to all these questions lead to a better understanding of the complexities and uncertainties and therefore will help leaders formulate an optimized strategy and action plan to successfully drive an organization forward within this environment.

Successful strategies are those that enable an organization to navigate the complexities and uncertainties that have caused, and will continue to cause, major disruptions. There are more and more drivers in the system with the power to influence outcomes, and high performance is how to transform these drivers in a unifying way in support of a particular objective. There has never been a more important time for organizations and management teams to find new ways to adapt and react in more thoughtful, strategic, and future-proofed ways. The application of scenario planning as a management tool enables organizations to deal with this kind of tangled, fast-moving future.

CASE STUDY
ACGME (Creating New Innovative Solutions)

The Accreditation Council for Graduate Medical Education (ACGME) is responsible for overseeing preparation of future physician specialists and subspecialists who serve the American public. ACGME is a not-for-profit organization that has three units focused, respectively, on accreditation, recognition, and initiatives to improve health care and population health. ACGME is headquartered in Chicago, United States, and has 230 employees.[5]

WHY AND HOW SCENARIO PLANNING WAS USED

ACGME was contemplating the future of medical care for the students who were being awarded accreditations or sponsoring related activities. The future is critical to the council as its programs were accrediting students who would not just practise now but also in the future, so understanding changing needs was critical to success. Accordingly, ACGME set out a mission to "address the range of future uncertainties in health care and graduate medical education" and used scenario planning to assist them, with a particular focus on strategic risk management and understanding those external risks that could change the evolving needs of the system. The scenario planning process consisted of three phases:

1. Over 100 preliminary interviews were conducted to survey medical professionals on the future of health care delivery. It was felt that the best way to get insights about the future would be from those in the system itself.

2. The group collected interview notes and developed four "varied [and] plausible" scenarios along two axes consistent with traditional scenario planning methods.

3. ACGME conducted two workshops: the first consisted of 50 leaders in health care who spent three days working with each of the four scenarios; the leaders developed a "U.S. health care system" that would flow logically from the circumstances in each scenario. The second workshop required the board of ACGME to use the scenarios and health systems designed in the first workshop to describe the educational systems that would support the models developed for each scenario and how ACGME's strategies could support that educational system.

ORGANIZATIONAL BENEFITS AND RESULTS

ACGME created a strategic plan, originating from the workshops, with the aim to support physicians who may practice in numerous different fields, since the scenarios outlined a future where medical physicians from across disciplines would be required to interact more to solve complex problems. The scenarios also resulted in a refined strategy with one of ACGME's pillars in their resulting strategic plan being updated to include "enhance interprofessional team-based care" as a main objective for the future.

Finally, the scenarios highlighted the ever-changing career market where individuals seek greater flexibility in their jobs. So to ensure medicine attracts the best and brightest, ACGME began to rethink the terms "physical specialist and subspecialists" to broaden the definitions for which they are accredited.

By leveraging scenarios, the organization was able to understand the implications of new risks emerging in this space, stress-test and validate the existing strategy, and provide *new innovative solutions* broadening the accreditation process.[6,7]

MACRO FACTORS CHANGING THE WORLD

At the World Economic Forum in Davos in 2018, Canadian prime minister Justin Trudeau said, "The pace of change has never been this fast, yet it will never be this slow again."[8] With eight billion people on the planet, and steadily increasing velocity and volatility, there has never been a more complex, uncertain, but also exciting, time as today. So it's that much more important to manage change to maintain success.

As you unpack uncertainty and complexity in more detail, eight main macro forces are having a fundamental and far-reaching impact on how we live our lives and how business is conducted. Consider these both as risks and also opportunities for the future:

1. **Geopolitics:** There are many forces shaping the geopolitical landscape today, including the recent nationalization trends we've seen across the world with the push against globalization, nations looking for opportunities to manufacture and create jobs locally, and a trend to be less connected and reliant on the global system. Brexit is a case in point, and the election of Donald Trump as

the 45th U.S president, who won in part on a nationalization agenda, is another. We've also seen the rise of China as a new economic superpower, shifting influence away from the United States. It is expected that by 2028 China will overtake the United States as the biggest economy and the largest superpower on the planet. Emerging economies, such as Iran, Egypt, Pakistan, Saudi Arabia, Taiwan, Thailand, Mexico, and Brazil, are now growth markets and global demographics will change as a consequence. Commodity prices are another factor driven by geopolitics with significant consequences for places like Canada and the United States impacted by OPEC flooding the market with additional crude oil production.

2. **Technology, Digital, and Innovation:** You cannot go very far in business today without the word *digital* coming up in conversation, as either part of a strategy or as a priority. Digital is critical to the success of any organization, but it's also incredibly hard to stay ahead of the constantly evolving innovations and the required upgrading of technical skills. Some of the important technologies to watch for in the coming years will be artificial intelligence, advanced analytics, augmented reality, virtual reality, blockchain, Internet of Things (IOT), mobility (work anytime, anywhere, on any device), nanotechnology, emotionally intelligent machines, and big data. These technologies could drastically change how products are produced and consumed and also how we collaborate and make decisions in an increasingly connected world. The transformation of digital banking in the last several years is a case in point as to how rapidly things are changing. The CEO of Bank of America, Brian Moynihan, has said, "Digital banking is a key strategy to millennial consumers" and also indicated that the bank was able to cut 100,000

jobs in less than a decade since it began reducing costs by focusing on a digital strategy in 2008.[9]

3. **Climate Change and the Green Revolution:** Climate change is an existential threat to our planet and the human race, and one that is being taken very seriously by governments and organizations across the world. The emergence of wind, solar, hydroelectric, and thermal as alternative sources of energy could have dramatic impacts on traditional fossil fuel industries like oil, gas, and coal. The world is getting warmer, and if predictions are correct, the surface temperature of the planet will increase by 3 to 5 degrees by 2100. The sustainability and social licence of organizations have never been more important issues for leadership teams to consider if they hope to maintain performance on the stock market, but they are also factors in the broader success of organizations at large.

4. **New Human Behaviours:** Human behaviour is now being shaped by social media and the web. As we all know, people feel restless and uneasy if they don't regularly look at their phones or are not constantly connected. According to research from RescueTime, a firm that created a time management app for iOS and Android, humans spend an average of three hours and 15 minutes on their phones every day.[10] Furthermore, we are interrupted by a daily volume of information that is affecting our cognition, and some researchers believe this barrage could permanently change the cognition of our brains. Another behavioural trend is that the millennial workforce brings with it new attitudes, different expectations, and new ways of working that organizations have done a poor job of embracing. There are also changing family structures, with more single-person households, lower birth rates

in the developed world, and cultural convergence driven partly by greater mobility.

With the emergence of the "prosumer"—rather than mere consumers—people today can significantly affect the success or failure of brands, especially through involvement on social media. The growth of distributed energy resources (DERs), which are small-scale technologies that allow consumers to generate power and, if they choose, sell the power back to the grid, is emerging as a trend as well, a move away from the traditional top-down power-supply system of the last several decades, according to the International Energy Agency (IEA). The IEA also indicates that the growth of rooftop solar has been massive in some countries. For example, in Australia more than 20 percent of households are equipped with solar.[11]

5. **Population Growth and Urbanization:** The planet is expected to have 9.7 billion people by 2050, with urbanization expected to increase by 66 percent by 2050 (increasing by 50,000 per day), which will reshape how cities expand and function in the future.[12] The UN states that there are now 33 of what are called "megacities," with populations of more than 10 million, many of which exist in China and India. (By 2060, 66 percent of the middle class will live in Asia.)[13] High birth rates in less developed countries and lower birth rates in the developed world will continue, and the growth of the middle class will create all kinds of new needs, requirements, and opportunities.[14]

6. **Agriculture and Food by Design:** With population growth and rising incomes, global demand is putting pressure on the agribusiness industry to grow and innovate. Agriculture will need

to feed 40 percent more people, produce 70 percent more food, and use only 10 percent more land. As income levels rise globally, diets in developing countries also evolve. In addition, new technologies and innovations are driving industry transformation and disrupting the market landscape. More than $4.6 billion has been invested in "agtech" in the past five years with drones, apps, and software becoming as commonplace as seed, chemicals, and equipment. It is estimated that 50 percent of the current workforce processes are expected to be automated by agtech and AI through innovations in technology, analytics, and business models.

7. **Health Reimagined:** The health care industry has been going through a transformation for years and that is expected to continue for the foreseeable future. Governments and the private sector will be forced to rethink health care because of factors like the aging population; global pandemics; changing life expectancy (in China, for example, it will rise to 80 years by 2050); increased access to water, which means people will live longer; and the growth of obesity and mental health issues. The emergence of telemedicine, increased spending on drugs, and innovative private insurance models will also be factors transforming how health care works. Digital tools such as app-based biometric self-assessments, online scheduling, virtual triage, and wearables such as digital watches that monitor your heart rate and other biometrics will be increasingly important. As a result, hospitals, physicians, and personal care networks will need to revisit their operating models to incorporate digital— whether through virtual waiting rooms, automation, real-time health monitoring, shared services, or other digital platforms. According to "OECD Policy Responses to COVID-19," the global pandemic has led governments to collaborate with telecommunications providers

to access geolocation data that can track the movement of people. For example, the German telecommunications provider Deutsche Telekom is providing anonymized "movement flows" data of its users to the Robert Koch Institute, a German government agency and research institute responsible for disease control and prevention.[15]

8. **Resilient Supply Chains:** In a globalized world, the interconnectedness of supply chains is expected to continue to expand, although there could be some rebalancing, with an increase in domestic production of essential products deemed strategic in nature to the functioning of a country. The flow of goods, information, and capital are constantly changing, and the rise of online supermarket chains like Amazon has never been more prevalent and powerful. According to bigcommerce.com, Amazon now controls 50 percent of the e-commerce market in the United States, which is more than its top three competitors combined.[16] Demand planning at the end of the cycle will continue to be critical to success, we can expect further coemption and pricing pressures as consumers look for cheaper products, outsourcing back to insourcing might emerge, and shortened and more complex product lifecycles will be important to watch.

These eight macro forces represent a business and market context that is ever changing and that must be carefully monitored by companies if they hope to stay ahead and avoid unexpected surprises. Some macro forces will have more relevance to a particular organization and others less, but what's important is to assess, prioritize, and incorporate these into the scenario planning thinking. These macro forces act as a starting point to understanding the complex world in which every company operates, and they can help leaders build a strategy that will successfully mitigate risks and seize opportunities that lie ahead.

RESPONDING TO COMPLEXITY AND UNCERTAINTY

How can scenario planning help leaders deal with complexity and uncertainty? The research on the topic is extensive. Philip R. Walsh specifically describes the link between environmental uncertainty and scenario planning. When a firm finds itself in a changing environment, it must process all available information and create strategies to deal with all the changes.[17] *Adaptive* organizations are those in which management is encouraged to identify changes in the environment through scenarios and make changes to the strategy. Leadership teams, though, by nature have limits to their ability to process complex information.

Scenarios arrange the possibilities in a structured and simple form that facilitates decision-making. By addressing the effects of variables through scenario planning, a firm develops insights and intelligence that helps it formulate strategy in a shifting environment.

In the face of adversity during COVID-19, Zoom video communication has responded exceptionally well as millions of remote workers look for technology to support ongoing operations. Despite some early security issues, Zoom is seen as easy to use, reliable, fun, and free (using the basic plan). Zoom's revenues for its first fiscal quarter in 2020 were up 169 percent from the same period a year earlier, with a profit of $27 million, up from $198,000 in 2019.[18] The CEO, Eric Yuan, predicted that videoconferencing would become a mainstream service, and since COVID-19, it certainly has.

Some view external uncertainty as an accelerating phenomenon due to the disruption caused by digital technology, deregulation, new business models, and the threat of new competitive entrants. This constant change increases the scrutiny of the strategic planning process, raising questions about how to ensure the strategy remains relevant in turbulent times, but also how long-term certainty in the strategic approach can be built in—how to "future-proof" the strategy.[19] For example, the media industry is facing a huge disruption as the growth of online media puts pressure on traditional print publications. New approaches to web design, search engine optimization, pay-per-click, social media marketing, and content marketing are constantly being introduced. There has never been a more important time for this sector to be creative, consider uncertainty, build in options, and perform strategic analysis.

There is one important danger of which leaders must be aware. Once external uncertainties and risks have been identified through scenario planning, internal issues could interfere with acting on them. Business leaders face internal complexities that, as they grow, cause organizations to become less capable of identifying and mitigating the impact of external risks. Especially in large organizations, vulnerabilities grow as the organizations become more complex and, according to Eric Bonabeau, chief scientific officer at San Francisco's Telepathy Labs, complexity breeds fragility. When companies expand, adopt new technologies, and adjust organizational structures, performance management systems, and governance frameworks, they become less flexible and nimble, and leaders may be distracted from the intelligence they were given during the scenario planning process. If some of these threats, complexities, and uncertainties become a reality, they can, in turn, trigger internal flaws in the organization.[20]

Part of the strategy of dealing with both internal complexity and external uncertainty is the ability to understand the information to which a firm has access via the scenario planning process. But it's essential that leaders are able to process it in such a way that they can understand and react to key driving forces, insights, threats, and opportunities. According to the World Economic Forum, the entire digital universe is expected to reach 44 zettabytes by 2020, which is 40 times more bytes than there are stars in the observable universe. The processing of this mass of data is dealt with in Chapter 7 on artificial intelligence; artificial intelligence represents an important capability that organizations need to take seriously.[21]

CASE STUDY
Rolls-Royce Holdings plc (Stress-Testing Your Strategy)

A multinational engineering company that designs, manufactures, and distributes power systems, Rolls-Royce is the world's second-largest maker of aircraft engines, 16th-largest defence contractor, as of 2018 when measured by defence revenues, and has major businesses in marine propulsion and the energy sector. Rolls-Royce reported revenues in 2019 of over $20 billion USD and employs more than 50,000 personnel worldwide. The company is headquartered in London, England.

WHY AND HOW SCENARIO PLANNING WAS USED

Rolls-Royce's stock had fallen more than 50 percent between 2014 and 2015 due to a cyclical decline in airline orders, the slow growth rate of the Chinese economy, and the end of the commodities boom, which simultaneously impacted the corporate jet, marine, and energy business.

A new CEO, Warren East, appointed in 2015, approached Oxford University to run a scenario planning executive education course. The following goal was devised: "Catalogue significant factors that might affect Rolls-Royce by the year 2040, and develop a set of strategic questions." East was eager to learn and plan for the future by understanding multiple possible and plausible realities.

Having the right stakeholders involved was critical to success. The process consisted of 25 mid- and senior-level executives, selected from different business units, functions, and locations to participate in the three-day workshop, which consisted of four phases:

1. Undertake individual research on pre-assigned and personally chosen topics.

2. Formulate groups to compile research in order to develop draft scenarios.

3. Finalize three detailed yet broad scenarios as a cohort.

4. Critique and review the scenarios and develop four strategic questions to ask about the future.

ORGANIZATIONAL BENEFITS AND RESULTS

The management team used the Oxford University workshop to share learning outcomes throughout the company as the three scenarios became a starting point for their 2016 strategic planning process. The organization *stress-tested and validated their investments* against the scenarios. All investment proposals were required to consider the scenarios, as well as how to mitigate or exploit dynamics of the scenario.

Experiences of rapid changes in market dynamics had propelled revenue problems for Rolls-Royce in the past. However, with future scenarios outlined, the organization's ability to nimbly respond improved dramatically, and Rolls-Royce executives benefited from more formally being able to *assess uncertainty.* In addition, certain cases in the scenarios have become the reality today—for example, one scenario predicted a new world order in which China and India leveraged technology to rival the United States, and countries would be forced to adapt, a situation that has largely occurred.

> In fact, by 2020, it became clear that China had caught up with the United States in technological power.[22]

BUSINESS RESILIENCE

While uncertainty and complexity can create risk for an organization, it can also create opportunity. From a risk perspective it's important to constantly consider ways to assess external and internal challenges to an organization to help make better and more informed decisions for mitigation strategies. The "King of Beers," Budweiser, realizing beer sales at pubs and restaurants were threatened during the outbreak of COVID-19, pivoted and announced it would "begin producing and distributing bottles of hand sanitizer to accommodate the growing needs across the United States." I'm not sure whether Budweiser called what it was doing "scenario planning," but the way the company was attuned to the external world, understood the coming threats and uncertainties, and pivoted illustrates the kind of insight and flexibility that are important outcomes of scenario planning. As Eric Bonabeau points out, leaders need to spot vulnerabilities and fix them before something major occurs and "design out" the weaknesses through business resilience.[23]

The frequency of scenario planning can also be important, especially when an organization finds itself coping with severely demanding circumstances. One example is the way Emarsys, an international, cloud-based marketing and customer engagement platform, dealt with the COVID-19 pandemic. Chris Ortega, the company's director of finance for the Americas, said the organization increased its meetings from monthly to weekly, daily, sometimes even hourly, to be ready to respond to its customers' needs. "Our scenario planning looks at business drivers and how changes affect revenue, cash, and customer attrition," said Ortega. "We were doing all that planning in Excel, but I realized we can be 10 or even 20 times more efficient and effective if we have scenario planning technology." Emarsys is now investing in custom-designed planning and analysis technology so it can become faster and even more agile.[24]

Business resilience can be characterized by six vital components: portfolio, capital and financial, operational, market, stakeholder, and talent management. Success for an organization that wants to manage risk and uncertainty involves considering risks within each of these areas and preparing strategies to react and adapt to each one. It's important to understand that while this business resilience model does not paint a picture of what multiple futures look like, which is what scenario planning does, it does offer some insights into the areas of focus with regard to risk, as well as strategies to mitigate those risks, that form part of the scenario planning process.

Specific subfactors within each of these six components, which should be assessed in terms of risk and resilience, can be summarized as follows:

1. **Portfolio:** Opportunities to capitalize on transactions and maximize returns
   - Reallocation of capital to optimize returns
   - Divesting of underperforming or noncore assets
   - Opportunistic transactions
   - Partnerships to share capital and costs (such as joint ventures)

2. **Capital and financial:** Long-term financing strategies, minimizing bad debt, and capital efficiency gains
   - Flexible long-term financing
   - Achievable debt covenants supported by robust cash flows
   - Strong working capital performance
   - Robust management of legacy liabilities

3. **Operational:** Adaptive and proactive approaches to operating risks and costs
   - Greater management of operating costs
   - Optimization of supply chain management
   - Management of operational risks
   - Innovation of operating models
   - Proactive investment in technology

4. **Market:** Revenue/sales risk management through customer, product, market, competition, and pricing analysis
   - Management of revenue, product, pricing, and sales risk
   - Management of customer, market, and competition
   - Management of product and pricing
   - Regular use of market and tracing data to align customer-facing activity
   - Investment in disruptive technology

5. **Stakeholder:** Active engagement and alignment with stakeholder equity groups
   - A clear vision for the business supported by market trends and organizational capabilities
   - Active engagement and alignment with equity, financial, regulatory, supplier, and other stakeholder groups

6. **Talent management:** Culture, leadership, capability development, succession planning, and retention strategies
   - Increased investment in employee skills and capabilities
   - Active cultivation of an organizational culture
   - Stable and accountable leadership
   - Active headcount management
   - Salary and bonus adjustments

By taking each of the six components and subcomponents and understanding the risks and opportunities, organizations can better prepare for future possibilities. This action can be described as future-proofing the organizations, which includes developing shock absorbers for possible macro forces that could affect the organization.

In an increasingly complex and uncertain world, businesses need to consider several critical questions to enhance resilience and risk management, including these:

- How can my strategy remain relevant in turbulent times?
- How do I create more certainty in my business?
- How is the company identifying internal and external risks and adapting to disruptive environments?
- How can risks be mitigated?
- How does the company's position in the market, size, ownership structure, and other potential characteristics affect its strategic outcomes?
- Are there specific components of the resiliency framework that are more or less important to monitor for risks and preparedness?
- How can the organization use aspects of scenario planning to build greater business resilience?

Understanding external risks, and being strategically prepared to mitigate them, forms part of the scenario planning process described in a later chapter. Scenario planning offers a tool to help organizations be more resilient and, by considering the six components of resilience I listed above as part of the process, construct strategies to react and adapt under each scenario in a more balanced and all-encompassing way. Successful scenario planning isn't only about developing and discussing the scenarios; it's also what you strategically decide to do in each individual case. There may be times when leaders decide it's best to leave a strategy unchanged regardless of what scenario planning suggests they do.

SYSTEMS THINKING

Systems thinking is a holistic approach to analysis that focuses on the way that different parts of a system integrate and interrelate, and how systems operate within the context of larger systems. In a world of increasing access to information, thinking becomes decisively important, and the ability to process the information becomes essential to success. Systems thinking is another concept of relevance to scenario planning that enables the perception of reality from many different points instead of one.[25] Good leaders who can use systems thinking have cognitive, emotional, and social intelligence. It's more than just identifying risks and macro drivers; it's understanding why, how, and what it means to the organization.

Systems thinking helps organizations understand deeper patterns lying behind external events, including interrelations, processes of changes, and context. Leaders can develop their systems thinking skills by learning and improving their knowledge of systems philosophy—tying nicely to one of the main benefits of scenario planning, which is organizational learning—and also through work experience and developing social and emotional competencies.

Uncertainty is disadvantageous to maintaining balance and organizational performance, but some leaders seek uncertainty and complexity and prosper in that environment; they become more, not less, innovative in uncertain environments. This ability can occur first by positioning a firm to influence the environment, and second by allowing managers to choose their environment and create opportunities. Organizations can seek to control environments by increasing their power over selected segments of that environment, adapting by designing structures and practices to permit responses. When this happens, equilibrium is achieved, reducing threats to a firm's performance.[26]

Some critical questions organizations can ask themselves about the maturity of their systems thinking approach are these:

- Are we framing the problem as a pattern of behaviours?
- Do we understand the internal and external actors and their behaviours?
- Do we understand the context of different relationships?
- Do we understand causality and how behaviour gets initiated?
- Do we understand the complexity in the system and what causes it?
- Are we thinking holistically in a strategy development process?
- Have we designed our organization for the future?

Scenario planning also enables organizations to think about the wider system components that can influence performance by

- Placing a greater focus on external risks, threats, uncertainties, and trends
- Placing a greater focus on thinking and imagining the future
- Placing a greater emphasis on causal connections between key drivers of change
- Encouraging leaders not to build static, one-dimensional strategies, but flexile ones that can pivot based on how different future scenarios play out

People who are naturally curious and think from a system perspective understand the world in which the organization operates and its interrelationships in completely different and illuminating ways when compared to others, which can help position strategies for success.

INTELLIGENT ORGANIZATIONS

Scenario planning helps to create an intelligent organization in four ways:

- By applying a greater focus on external risks, threats, uncertainties, trends, and drivers
- By focusing on thinking and imagining the future
- By placing an emphasis on causal connections between key drivers of change
- By discouraging leaders from building static one-dimensional strategies and instead creating flexible strategies that can pivot based on different future scenarios playing out

Markus Schwaninger focuses on the concept of *intelligent organizations* that are able to adapt to changing situations, influence and shape their environment, make a contribution to the sustainability of the market in which the organization is embedded, and find new playing fields. Intelligent organizations, he argues, deal with business complexity very effectively in their variety and multiplicity.[27]

According to Daan van Beek, traditional organizations make decisions occasionally; intelligent organizations make decisions constantly and at all levels, even beyond the boundaries of the organization. He outlines how customer-oriented strategies are the key to intelligent organizations. For example, Amazon's CEO, Jeff Bezos, credits his firm's trillion-dollar success to one "secret sauce": "an obsessive-compulsive focus" on customers over competitors. These capabilities require excellent integration of systems; very open cultures; high-performing leaders; and a proactive sharing of information, knowledge, responsibilities, and results.[28]

Part of becoming an intelligent organization is also the ability of senior management to adapt their mental models. Scenario planning can influence management cognition and support organizational learning with broader mental models, helping a firm make better decisions. Riccardo Vecchiato, associate professor of strategic management at London's Kingston University, describes the chief benefit of scenario planning as a tool to change assumptions and enhance strategic flexibility within the organization by scanning, coding, updating, and understanding the future as it unfolds.[29]

Senior leaders can suffer from large egos and an inability to change mental models in an environment that is rapidly changing, possibly resulting in organizational inertia. Leadership beliefs are made up of mental models and strategic assumptions, but scenario planning can influence those strongly held beliefs.

The process of developing worst-case/best-case scenarios forces leaders outside of their comfort zones. For example, leaders of a multinational that owns supermarket chains might have to confront the reality of their customer base abruptly dropping by 50 percent because of an external event beyond their control, like Amazon suddenly becoming a chief competitor. The easy and comfortable reactions of the past would no longer work. Scenario planning turns an organization's world upside down, challenging leaders to abandon traditional mental models and think through some crazy, but plausible, futures.

Critical questions leaders can ask themselves to evaluate whether they are part of an intelligent organization include these:

- Are we integrated in our thinking?
- Are we multidimensional in our thinking?
- Are we reactive or proactive in our thinking?
- Are the components that influence our organization dynamically interrelated?

STRATEGIC ANTICIPATION

Strategic anticipation is an organization's capability to identify, understand, and react to future uncertainties, thereby mitigating their impacts and seizing on any commercial advantages. According to David Reilly, the British digital marketing strategist, the required capabilities vital for strategic anticipation include the following:

1. Employing a structured and disciplined team approach to monitoring and identifying potential threats and risks
2. Identifying your changing customer needs and emerging technology requirements
3. Building a multidisciplinary team with regard to knowledge, collaboration, and inputs
4. Testing the future by creating in-house innovation labs to validate new ideas

Like the model proposed by George Burt and Kees van der Heijden in 2003, organizations typically evolve to an *"anticipation,"* or scenario planning–based, approach when they are challenged in a particular sector or market, when leaders must continue to compete to stay viable.[30]

However, scenario planning is valuable only up to a point. As complexity and uncertainty increase beyond what is manageable, its value diminishes. Organizations typically start with more "reactive" ways of dealing with the external and internal environments, but as they mature, more "proactive" management tools are employed, such as scenario planning. These types of tools allow for greater strategic anticipation, enhanced business resilience, and, in general, a more intelligent approach to challenges. But when the market becomes grievously volatile, the sheer volume of information to process, assess, and adapt to becomes overwhelming and there is no longer a basis to forecast the future. At a time like this, the value of scenario planning diminishes, and a firm may have to return to a reactive strategy.

Success in any organization is about finding the right management tool that helps deal with the specific circumstances it faces at that point in time; it's not a case of one-size-fits-all. For example, a small start-up in a very stable sector does not necessarily need complex strategy tools. However, a start-up operating in Silicon Valley in the biotech sector likely does, as the speed of innovation and change is immense, and multiple shifting external factors need to be dealt with.

One thing is certain: complexity and uncertainty are not going away, and if anything, they will become even more intense in many sectors across the globe. With the onset of the 2020 global pandemic and the accompanying crashes in crude oil prices, changes in passenger travel, and political instability in many regions, there has never been a more challenging time for business leaders. "If digital disruption was a dress rehearsal for your business model's digitization," said futurist Anders Sörman-Nilsson, "COVID19 became the burning platform."[31]

The job of a leader is to formulate strategies that are agile, can quickly pivot, and remain strategically flexible despite market volatility. The ability of leaders to stretch their mental models, to transform how organizations operate and grow, is more important than ever. Leaders need to be able to consider internal and external factors when strategic planning. Gone are the days of static strategies. If a business wants to remain successful and competitive in a changing market, it needs to be able to dynamically and quickly change its strategy when necessary.

In summary, the literature is extensive in addressing the importance of complexity and uncertainty and the specific role that scenario planning plays in mitigating impacts by enabling greater systems thinking, risk management, business resilience, more intelligent organizations, and strategic anticipation. Scenario planning offers a way of blending multiple theories, tools, and techniques together to help make sense of all this change and the macro forces that are buffeting our world.

■ ■ ■

SUMMARY KEY POINTS

- The common definition of complexity is a measure of the total number of properties transmitted by an object and detected by an observer.
- Uncertainty is defined as doubt. An example of an uncertainty is when the economy is going bad and causing everyone to get concerned about what will happen next.
- Both complexity and uncertainty in organizations and markets are increasing because of a variety of political, economic, social, technological, environmental, and legal factors.
- There are eight macro forces shaping our world, with varying degrees of impact on an organization, that should be considered when developing strategies.
- Adaptive organizations are those in which management is encouraged to identify changes in the environment through scenarios and quickly make changes to the strategy.
- Business resilience is the strategic organizational capability to mitigate and adapt to disruptive and destructive threats, reshape environments, and survive both foreseen and unforeseen risks.
- Business resilience can be characterized by six key components: portfolio, capital and financial, operational, market, stakeholder, and talent management.
- Systems thinking is a holistic approach to analysis that focuses on the way different parts of the system integrate and interrelate, and how systems work overtime and within the context of larger systems.

- Intelligent organizations are able to adapt to changing situations, influence and shape their environment, and make a contribution to the sustainability of the larger organization as a whole.
- The concepts of adaptive organizations, business resilience, systems thinking, and intelligent organization offer different ways organizations can deal with complexity and uncertainty to be successful.
- Scenario planning enables organizations to deal with complexity and uncertainty to a point, but as true ambiguity takes hold, its value as a management tool diminishes.

CHAPTER 3

STEP-BY-STEP GUIDE TO SCENARIO PLANNING

"A plan is only a scenario, and almost by definition, it is optimistic. As a result, scenario planning can lead to a serious underestimate of the risk of failure."

—DANIEL KAHNEMAN, PSYCHOLOGIST AND ECONOMIST

In the mid-1990s, British Airways had made the transition from an unprofitable national carrier to a publicly listed company that was the largest global passenger airline in the world, employing more than 53,000 people and reporting a turnover of 7 billion GBP. It had also begun generating profits at a time when the international airline industry as a whole had lost $10 billion USD. Although the outlook was promising, the company's chief economist, DeAnne Julius, knew that it was dangerous to assume that the strategies working today would still be valid in the future. So he approached the chairman's committee with a suggestion to begin scenario planning for the organization. The leadership team approved the process but noted it would be taken on as an "experiment"; if it proved useful, it would be adopted into the 1995 strategic planning process.

The scenario planning process was conducted in two phases: scenario development and scenario workshops. For phase one, a group of employees from across the organization began to develop a list of "significant exter-nal issues" that were facing the airline over the coming decade. For phase two, many workshops were conducted so participants could evaluate the scenarios and voice their opinions to stress-test them, gradually building a robust picture of the future.

A number of benefits were achieved through the process. For example, customer service representatives used the scenarios to seek out better links between the airline and its passengers. This was not an original intention, but a customer service agent's interest in the planning process sparked a new opportunity for improvement.

During the scenario development component of the process, the lead-ing team used internal sources for research (such as employees in different departments). This directly led to further sharing and engagement about the company's future and buy-in on the part of employees.

Certain areas of the company's operations were not originally factored in to the planning process but arose when employees from these areas asked questions and stress-tested the scenarios against their own group's business goals. The Pacific Region of the company revaluated its plan for the area after hearing scenarios of potential instability in Asia. The new plan placed a greater emphasis on risk management.

In summary, the fact that front-line employees were involved in the process of developing the scenarios meant strategies were better validated and more in touch with the business realities facing British Airways. Also, the translation of the scenarios into organizational tactics occurred more easily as employees eagerly began using and adapting to the outcomes of the process.[1]

■ ■ ■

Chapter 2 defined uncertainty and complexity and examined how it cre-ates all kinds of challenges for leaders in organizations to manage in the face of pressures to sustain and improve business results. It also addressed the kinds of macro forces that are creating uncertainty and introduced existing concepts such as resilience, intelligent organizations, and strategic anticipation as "theoretical" concepts to overcoming these challenges. In this chapter, I explain the more practical approach to scenario planning, which I have boiled down to six important steps, starting with a definition of the scope and identification of major stakeholders through to monitoring signposts and executing strategies. This process, and the hands-on tools provided, can be applied at any level of an organization from a multinational global corporation to a specific capital project within a business unit of a company. Scenario planning can be broad or very focused, depending on the specific needs of the company involved and the problem that needs to be solved.

THE PROCESS OF SCENARIO PLANNING

There are several well-known articles by various researchers that describe the process of using scenario planning within an organization, with perhaps the most famous by the author and scenario planning pioneer Paul Schoemaker. He describes the steps involved in scenario planning in some detail. He also notes that when contemplating the future, it's important to consider three types of knowledge within the scenario planning process:

- Things we know we know
- Things we know we don't know, and
- Things we don't know we don't know

Schoemaker goes a step further, providing insights into how many scenarios should be developed, the focus of each one, integrating them into a firm's strategy, and, importantly, outlining the different levels of scenarios within an organization.[2]

Scenarios need to be tightly integrated into the strategic planning process to be successful. In large complex organizations, like the oil and gas company Shell, entire teams are established with the sole purpose of supporting scenario planning. Shell's teams narrow the range of uncertainty and complexity through a funnel-like process. On the left side, the funnel is wide, and Shell seeks to understand social, political, economic, environmental, and technological drivers through scenarios. Then they assess what the market wants through customer intelligence and examine what value the company's competitors provide. As the information narrows through the funnel, uncertainty is steadily eliminated and Shell understands how it can differentiate itself from its competitors.[3]

Let's outline my proposed six steps of scenario planning in more detail, explaining activities, deliverables, tools, accelerators, and essential questions users should consider while executing the process. This approach is based on my years of consulting experience in a variety of sectors at Ernst & Young and Accenture, helping clients solve their most pressing strategic problems. The approach builds on what others have developed, with refinements made through trial and error.

1. DEFINE THE SCOPE AND IDENTIFY MAJOR STAKEHOLDERS

Experience shows that formulating scenarios fosters a strategic dialogue among stakeholders that can result in unexpected findings.

In the first step of the scenario development process, the project's scope and time frame should be defined. The goal is to clarify the strategic problem that stakeholders want to address by using scenarios and to determine the level of scenario planning that should be performed. The key is for stakeholders to agree on a sharp, clear question that frames the scenario planning process by setting the time horizon and level of planning, formulating additional boundaries, and drawing up the project's structure. Time frames are dependent on a variety of factors, including rate of change within a particular sector, specific country elections, product lifecycles, and the behaviour of competitors.

KEY ACTIVITIES AND WORK PRODUCTS

- Identify core problem
  - The most effective way to reveal the core problem is through a series of structured interviews, allowing decision-makers and leaders to identify the issues they feel will shape the future of the organization. All leaders have concerns; the key is to uncover those concerns.
  - Stakeholder anxieties and unstructured concerns can typically be a good starting point for the scenario planning process.
  - Bringing leaders together in a workshop setting can help enable facilitators to listen and promote dialogue on the core problems. At this time it's important to have a clear definition of the problem as well as the need for a solution, putting the problem into a context, and having a written problem statement.

PROBLEM STATEMENT DEFINITION FRAMEWORK

A problem statement is a clear and concise description of an issue that needs to be solved by a problem-solving team. It describes the gap between the current level of performance and the desired future level of performance. A problem statement should not include possible root causes or solutions. Here is a rough guideline:

First, establish the need for a solution through a series of questions:

- What is the basic need (rational)?
- What is the want (emotional)?
- What is the (hidden) fear?
- What is the desired outcome?
- Who stands to benefit, and why?

Second, justify the need:

- Is the effort aligned with our business strategy, and why?
- What are the desired benefits for the firm and how will we measure them?

Third, contextualize the problem:

- What approaches have we tried and failed?
- What have others tried?
- What are the internal and external constraints on implementing a solution?

Fourth, write the problem statement:

- Are we facing one, or many, problems?
- What requirements must a solution meet?
- What information and language should be included in the problem statement?
- How will solutions be evaluated and success measured?

- Define focal questions
    - Based on a structured discussion, the essential questions about the future will be defined and serve as guidance for the scenario

analysis. The question itself will set the tone for the scenario analysis. Leadership involvement is critical in this process since the outcome will determine the strategic direction of the entire exercise. The facilitator should manage a logical process but encourage creativity and lateral thinking during the dialogue.

- It's also important to ask what kind of knowledge and information would be helpful for the organization to understand and to explore those gaps and opportunities. The knowledge and information are typically strategic in nature, and facilitators need to be careful to avoid getting bogged down.

- Confirm time horizon

  - Based on the focal question(s), a time horizon is set in terms of how far into the future to consider as part of the scenario development. When setting an appropriate horizon, stakeholders should visualize how quickly changes can happen and at what point in the future the focal question(s) can be adequately answered. For example, changes in the mining sector might take years, but in the technology sector, months.

  - It's sometimes helpful to look at the past 10 years and analyze what happened and what you wish you'd known then.

- Formulate boundaries

  - To make the scenarios more specific, additional boundaries should be specified. For example, is the team developing scenarios for the entire company or only for a specific business unit or capital project? Being clear about the scope informs the type of research involved and also identifies the stakeholders to engage.

  - Consider whether scenarios are being created at the global, country, or business or project-specific level based on the focal question you are trying to answer.

- Agree on the organizational resources that will be invested into the scenario development process.

- Confirm stakeholders
  - In order to develop coherent and plausible scenarios, a careful balance of internal and external stakeholders who can influence the focal question(s) should be identified and their behaviour studied.
  - Confirm who will have the most interest in the issues you are tackling given the potential impacts they face. Identify your allies.
  - Typical stakeholders are suppliers, customers, shareholders, employees, leaders, competitors, regulators, and government policy makers.
  - Consider defining the role you want the stakeholders to play, based on their interest in the scenario(s) and their perceived power position in the organization. A range of backgrounds and experiences makes for diverse perspectives.
  - It's important to have the right number of stakeholders. For example, when developing the scenarios, a smaller group of highly interested and engaged participants makes sense, but when sharing, getting feedback, refining, testing, and translating the results, a bigger group produces a greater awareness throughout the organization and a better chance of success when implementing the plan.

- Confirm structure of the scenario planning project
  - To deliver high-quality results, the project must be clearly structured. Topics to be addressed in a project plan include team composition, work streams, tooling, and research methods (e.g., interviews, workshops, desk research).

- Consider using external consultants to support the process where you have gaps.

HELPFUL TOOLS AND ACCELERATORS

Problem statement definition framework

Stakeholder list and assessment matrix

KEY QUESTIONS

- Who is the right person within the organization to facilitate the process?
- Have you prepared a powerful set of focal questions for the scenario planning process?
- Is the focal question a sector-/industry-specific question or not?
- Does the organization have the right stakeholders involved— those who will provide a diversity of perspectives and stretch the thinking of the group? (Specifically, you want stakeholders who will bring commitment, insights, experience, influence, and impact to the process.)
- Do the people involved have a stake in the future of the organization and are they respected for their views?
- Are the boundaries understood and realistic for the resources available to conduct the scenario planning exercise?
- Has a longer-term view been taken to avoid making this another strategic planning exercise?
- Is the organization clear about the level at which the scenarios are being created? (e.g., macro "world" and "country" scenarios for a multinational; local "business"-specific level for a single enterprise or business unit; or a specific "project" level within a business unit)
- Is the outside use of consulting support required?

- What ways can be adopted to build trust and relationships with the participants involved in the process?

CASE STUDY
U.S. Army Corps of Engineers (The Pitfalls of Involving Only a Small, Senior Team)

U.S. Army Corps of Engineers (USACE) is an engineering branch of the United States Army that oversees a wide range of public works throughout the world. USACE has over 37,000 civilian and military personnel, making it one of the largest public engineering, design, and construction agencies in the world. An example of some of the public work that USACE has executed is its hydroelectric projects, which provide over 24 percent of U.S. hydropower capacity.

WHY AND HOW SCENARIO PLANNING WAS USED

USACE's senior leaders outlined a twofold mission to a wide group of engineers to (a) foster strategic thinking in the organization and (b) produce a strategic plan to take into account future uncertainties. These senior leaders, making up the executive steering committee, conducted regular reviews and validation of the work produced throughout the exercise. The scenario planning process used by the group spanned more than two years and can be summarized in the following steps:

1. Defined the scope and boundaries of the scenario analysis, which were generally concerned with water resources in the United States.

2. Evaluated 124 external factors, deemed "important," that could affect water resources and mission areas of USACE.

3. Identified trends and uncertainties that were ranked based on importance and predictability. High importance and high predictability were identified as trends while high importance and low predictability were identified as uncertainties.

4. Developed four scenarios in a 2-by-2 matrix based on uncertainties expressed on a Y axis and X axis.

5. Defined core competencies of USACE today.

6. Defined key success factors for each of the scenarios and compared them to current competencies of the organization.

7. Set a future direction, which included goals and objectives.

ORGANIZATIONAL BENEFITS AND RESULTS

USACE noted that due to a small subgroup of their people being involved in the process, the organizational engagement was lower than expected. Executive leadership involvement was limited, and USACE noted that substitutes sent by the executive leadership did not provide nearly as much value for the process as the leaders of the organization would have.

USACE noted having more representatives from across the departments would have helped communicate the realism of the scenarios throughout the organization. Another take-away from the process was ensuring that "interim products and drafts [were] read closely and constructively by participants, outside experts and stakeholders" on an ongoing basis to ensure continuity throughout. USACE also critiqued the scope of the project and felt as though a "wider net [could] engage a broader cross section of USACE" and other stakeholders.

This case highlighted the importance of confirming the key stakeholders that need to be involved upfront in the define the scope and identify major stakeholders step of the process and guaranteeing top-down support for their involvement to ensure the required outcomes are achieved.[4,5]

2. EXPLORE THE INTERNAL AND EXTERNAL ENVIRONMENT

Exploring the environment is essential to reveal the elements underneath the visible surface of change.

In the second step, the internal and external environment is explored. As Pierre Wack, the cofounder of the Shell scenario team, emphasized, the most important step in the scenario planning process is the "breathing in" phase of truly understanding the current environment in all its uncertainty and complexity, and this creates the baseline for later "breathing out": building the scenarios and understanding what they mean.[6]

The goal is to identify external developments and forces that could be drivers of future change and have a large impact on the focal question. The external environment is explored from a macro as well as a local business environment perspective. Using well-known strategy tools and frameworks, such as Porter's five forces (see below) and the PESTEL (see below) analysis, all potential external sources of change outside of the organization are systematically uncovered and discussed.

KEY ACTIVITIES AND WORK PRODUCTS

- Scan the macro and micro business environment

- Go on a journey of discovery. Use the PESTEL analysis to identify forces of change in the macro- and micro-environments, including political, economic, social, technological, environmental, and demographic trends that could have a large impact on the organization's business model and future success.

- Consider, in some cases, in-depth interviews to really uncover the details of what is happening within the system. For example, if a firm decided it wanted to understand the policy direction of the country in which it operates, it would engage policy advisors within the company, or even externally, to hear what they believe are the drivers, trends, risks, and uncertainties.

- Use Porter's five forces framework to identify forces of change within the business environment. This analysis is focused on the behaviour of suppliers, buyers, and competitors, as well as the appearance of substitutes and new entrants.

- Assess the internal organizational environment using tools such as SWOT analysis, questionnaires, structured and unstructured interviews, and internal organizational data.

- Use various research methods such as expert interviews, brainstorming sessions, desk research, and surveys to generate a long list of potential forces.

- Use different thinking hats to expand the thinking process and ensure different perspectives are considered.

- Describe each force and trend within the environment

  - Include why and how it impacts your organization; for example, does it have a good, bad, or neutral impact on your business?

- Create master list

  - Create a master list by deleting all the items that are not relevant to the scope defined in Step 1. Focus on the critical forces and trends relating to the problems you are trying to solve.

HELPFUL TOOLS AND ACCELERATORS
PESTEL analysis

Porter's Five Forces

Competitive positioning framework

De Bono's Thinking Hats

PESTEL ANALYSIS

A PESTEL analysis is an acronym for a management tool that monitors and analyzes crucial external trends and macro forces that have an impact on an organization's success. It uses research methods such as expert interviews, brainstorming sessions, desk research, and surveys to generate a list of forces. The letters stand for Political, Economic, Social, Technological, Environmental, and Legal.[7]

- **Political Factors:** The relative stability of a government, as well as government policies—trade, fiscal, taxation, etc.—may have an effect on an organization or a specific industry.

- **Economic Factors:** Any forces affecting an economy will, in turn, have an impact on an organization and its profitability. These include interest rate fluctuations, employment or unemployment rates, raw material costs, and foreign exchange rates.

- **Social Factors:** These represent emerging trends in the social environment, helping stakeholders understand consumer needs and wants. They may include changing family demographics, education levels, cultural trends, attitudinal changes, and changes in lifestyles.

- **Technological Factors:** These factors take into account the rate of technological innovation and development that may affect a market or industry. They could include changes in digital or mobile technology, automation, and research and development. It's important not to focus solely on developments in digital technology at the expense of new methods of distribution, manufacturing, and logistics.

- **Environmental Factors:** These relate to the influence and impact of the surrounding environment, especially relevant since corporate sustainability responsibility (CSR) has become more important. Factors include climate, recycling procedures, carbon footprint, waste disposal, and sustainability.

- **Legal Factors:** An organization must understand its legal responsibilities within the territories in which it operates. Leaders must also be aware of any change in legislation and the impact this may have on business operations. Factors include employment legislation, consumer law, health and safety, and international trade regulation and restrictions.

Note: Political factors often intersect with legal factors. The important difference is that political factors are led by government policy and are open to lobbying and negotiation, whereas legal responsibilities must be met.

PORTER'S FIVE FORCES

Porter's Five Forces, developed by author and professor Michael Porter, is a framework for analyzing an organization's competitive environment. The market performance of a business is influenced by, for example,

1. The number and power of competitive rivals
2. Potential new market entrants
3. Suppliers
4. Customers
5. Substitute products

Any of these may influence an organization's market performance and outcomes. Porter's Five Forces can help leaders understand the challenges their organization faces so they can adjust their strategy to meet them.[8]

KEY QUESTIONS

- Have all the major driving forces in the external environment been identified? Including sector-specific forces?
- Have enough trends in each framework (PESTEL, Porter's Five Forces) been identified to ensure adequate balance?
- Have both primary and secondary research methods in the approach been considered?
- Does it make sense to commission an external research paper?
- In the description of each trend, has the team been able to make it simple and easy for a wide stakeholder group to understand?
- Does the organization truly understand the external threats?
- Does the organization have a good understanding of competitive positioning?
- Is there a diagram that can be constructed that helps with understanding the external environment?

- Have personal biases been avoided and assumptions and beliefs expanded?

CASE STUDY
Nan, Thailand (Creating a Sustainable Future With Low Carbon Tourism)

Nan is a small province (population 450,000) located in Thailand, which has a long history and unique culture that has made it a popular tourist destination for many years. Revenue from tourism in Nan was estimated at 1,882 million baht in 2015. Nan Municipality received an award from ASEAN Clean Tourist City Standard in 2018.

WHY AND HOW SCENARIO PLANNING WAS USED

Nan was focused on further developing as an "ecotourism city by promoting suitable natural resource management and conservation." In order to minimize negative dynamics of ecotourism, Nan used scenario planning to help prepare for this future development. The scenario planning Nan used consisted of numerous phases in the following order:

1. The team at Nan identified "a focal issue," which acted as a mission statement for the project.

2. Once a focal issue was selected, the team identified driving forces by using a "STEEP analysis" (Sociological, Technological, Economical, Environmental, and Political), similar to performing a PESTEL analysis.

3. With the information collected in the analysis, the issues were ranked based on importance and uncertainty.

4. The list of drivers (each of which were assigned uncertainty and importance ranks) was used to define scenario logics.

5. From scenario logics, the scenarios were developed. Select indicators that originated from the newly designed scenarios were monitored to evaluate how the scenarios expanded.

ORGANIZATIONAL BENEFITS AND RESULTS

Through the scenario planning exercise, Nan confirmed that low-carbon tourism could add value to the province and is crucial to the long-term sustainable development of the economy as well as the population's quality of life. Nan also noted that proactive engagement by the upcoming generation will have influence on the future development, ensuring there is a focus on low-carbon solutions.

From the scenario planning process, Nan was also able to designate certain indicators for a low-carbon tourism city, such as CO^2 per capita, proportion of renewable energy used, and share of waste recycling. Through conducting scenario planning, the province is now better able to understand the dynamics of a range of external factors by conceptualizing the entire picture. For example, deciding that foreign investment by fast food companies is an unattractive option for the province's future development due to the lack of environmental concern by these companies. Nan is now better prepared for the future. Its leaders *understand the external uncertainties and risks to manage, and the strategy has been tested and validated.*[9]

3. ANALYZE TRENDS, RISKS, AND UNCERTAINTIES

Predetermined elements are predictable; uncertainties are unpredictable. It's important to cast a critical eye on the external environment and start to document and analyze what could happen in the future.

This third step involves analyzing the list of external forces. The goal is to arrive at a small number of key uncertainties that are the driving forces of change in the external environment. Key uncertainties have the potential to shift the future in various ways. There are four steps to determining key uncertainties. First, identify the key uncertainties and forces. Second, remove external forces and developments that have low impact on the focal question. Third, group external forces and developments and conduct a cross-impact analysis. Finally, make a distinction between key trends (with a predictable impact) and key uncertainties (whose impact should be explored in a set of scenarios).

KEY ACTIVITIES AND WORK PRODUCTS

- Identify the key uncertainties and forces
  - Using various brainstorming techniques, identify uncertain forces (uncertainties) in the system that will have a large potential impact on the organization.
  - Consider outcomes of political elections, regulatory direction, policy changes, technology advances, and decisions on major capital projects as some examples. For each uncertainty, consider different potential outcomes that could be favourable, neutral, or unfavourable and document them in a table.
  - Think about the connection and integration between specific uncertainties in cases where they might exist.

- Remove forces with low potential impacts
  - Analyze the external forces and remove any that will have a low impact on the focal question and the organization's strategic agenda. These become distractions and complicate the scenario planning process.
- Cluster forces and trends
  - Group the remaining external forces, identified by logical trend clusters, on the basis of their interdependence and perspective.
  - Typically, a master list of 60 forces can be reduced to 10 to 15 force and trend clusters.
- Perform cross-impact analysis
  - Select potential key uncertainties by using a cross-impact analysis. For this exercise, analyze the causal relationships between all the trend groups.
  - Potential key uncertainties have a high cross-impact on other trend groups.

HELPFUL TOOLS AND ACCELERATORS

Brainstorming tools

Clustered trends and uncertainties

Cross-impact matrix

CLUSTER FORCES, TRENDS, AND UNCERTAINTIES

Forces, trends, and uncertainties should be clustered into similar groups with low-impact ones removed from the list. It's also important to make sure you don't have too many forces, trends, and uncertainties as that can create confusion and make the scenarios too complicated and frustrating. This approach helps a firm start to visualize a picture of the various scenarios that could become future realities. One technique that can help is using sticky notes on a white board to aid the grouping and clustering.

KEY QUESTIONS

- What are the most important certainties and uncertainties about the future? Including those that will be the most important to the particular sector involved?
- For each uncertainty, has a favourable, neutral, and unfavourable outcome been identified?
- Are there too many forces that become difficult to explain and use in the planning effort?
- Have appropriate grouping and clustering of trends been completed to simplify the picture?
- Is there a true understanding of the impacts of each market force and uncertainty?
- Are there broader stakeholders, both internal and external to the organization, that can provide alternative perspectives?
- Have forces with an inconsequential impact been removed?
- Have I spent enough time discussing the forces based on the complexity of the organization and focal question at hand?

4. BUILD SCENARIOS AND SIGNPOSTS (INTERNAL AND EXTERNAL)

Visualizing scenarios makes them come to life and clearly illustrates the implications of each one. Scenarios should be written like a story and engage the reader by being clear, relevant, plausible, and challenging.

In the fourth step, the scenario framework is set, and detailed scenarios and signposts are developed by the team. As Adam Kahane said in his book, *Transformative Scenario Planning*, "Scenario making is about acute perception, or better re-perception—becoming free of old perceptions and prejudices at the same time." A reliable way to create divergent scenarios is to picture key uncertainties on axes that frame the poles of what seems possible within the set time scale. A scenario frame, or matrix, forces the scenario writer to think more broadly about the future, describing alternative courses of action. The scenarios and signposts developed will be discussed with relevant stakeholders prior to discussion at the workshops.

It's important not to build too many scenarios. Although there is not a perfect number, three to four is recommended. One or two scenarios are more a forecast or a vision of the future, and more than four becomes too complex to define, explain, and understand.

KEY ACTIVITIES AND WORK PRODUCTS

- Build scenario frame
  - Identify scenario themes by putting all the positive elements in one bucket and the negative ones in another bucket.
  - Create divergent scenarios by picturing key uncertainties on axes that frame the poles of what seems possible within the set time scale.
  - Select the two most important independent key uncertainties to create a 2-by-2 scenario frame, which will result in four scenarios (the typical number). These uncertainties should have been ranked high on uncertainty and high on potential impact.

- Define their extreme positions—for example, globalization versus nationalization or centralization versus decentralization—and test their combination.
- The key uncertainties selected should have a low interdependence and preferably have a different perspective.

- Translate trends to scenario frame and identify signposts
  - Use the trend clusters to translate each one to the quadrants of the scenario frame. Not all trend clusters will be as relevant per quadrant.
  - Using all previously identified trend clusters helps to build a scenario framework that is challenging, plausible, consistent, relevant, and balanced.
  - Based on the scenario frame, identify the preceding signposts.

- Develop detailed stories
  - Describe a number of root causes for each scenario. Root causes are main reasons that the world might head in the direction of the scenario.
  - To structure the scenario stories, describe the implications in different layers of meaning. Drawing on the defined root causes and trend results, a narrative can be written for each scenario.
  - Build descriptors of the scenario, including a narrative of what happens, why it happens, and an explanation of future events and how they would unfold.

- Illustrate scenarios
  - Visually illustrate the scenarios to stimulate action and ideas. Scenarios should be accessible and understandable to people and documented in a way that will enable easy communication in the future.

- Possible illustration methodologies are cartoons, mock newspaper headlines from an imaginary future, or video documentaries that describe the scene. Consider including important charts (e.g., oil prices or another chart that brings a scenario to life) that help contextualize the key points.
- Create a name for each scenario that aligns with its features. The name should capture the essence of the scenario and help grab the attention of those who will read and adopt the information in the future. Consider metaphors.

- Check for relevance, plausibility, and consistency
  - Make sure the scenarios developed will be relevant to the stakeholders who will leverage them.
  - Make sure you validate each scenario for consistency and inconsistencies.
  - Read the storyline and make sure it comes across with impact and tells a compelling story.
  - Make sure the trend aligns with the scenario, and in cases where it does not, eliminate it from the scenario.
  - Ensure the outcomes of each uncertainty go together.
  - Ensure scenarios could actually happen and are not completely unrealistic.

- Identify additional research needs
  - In some cases, you might need to conduct further research on a particular topic to build out your knowledge of a trend or uncertainty. As an example, you may have to investigate specific technologies that could affect your business.
  - Consider quantitative analysis, including sales and financials, that can be pulled from the organization to go along with each

scenario, illustrating what could happen in each scenario in terms of the numbers.

HELPFUL TOOLS AND ACCELERATORS

Implication channel tool

Deductive scenario matrix

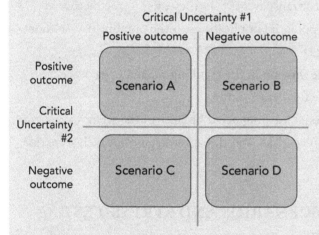

DEDUCTIVE SCENARIO MATRIX

Critical Uncertainty #1

	Positive outcome	Negative outcome
Positive outcome	Scenario A	Scenario B
Negative outcome	Scenario C	Scenario D

Critical Uncertainty #2

After risks and uncertainties are clustered into groups, descriptions of each of the four scenarios are created within either positive, negative, or mixed outcomes. These descriptions are checked for relevance, plausibility, and consistency; where gaps exist, additional research is conducted to fill in those gaps using primary and secondary research techniques.

Scenarios are created to mitigate key risks and uncertainties that exist in the market system and its landscape in order to manage transitions in this process.

KEY QUESTIONS

- Do the identified outcomes of each uncertainty go together?
- Do the scenarios really challenge and stretch the thinking and mental models of the organization based on the current dynamics playing out in the system?
- Are the developed scenarios plausible and relevant to the organization based on the current market situation? Can the scenarios be backed up by facts?
- Are the scenarios consistent?
- Are the scenarios versatile and flexible enough to meet the needs of the organization?
- Are the scenarios transparent? (Do they offer a true picture of the drivers and potential implications to the organization without hiding anything?)
- What factors are missing in the thinking related to each scenario that may require further thinking?
- Will organizational learning occur because of the scenarios?
- What critical issues, risks, and threats emerge from each scenario?

5. CONFIRM SCENARIOS AND STRESS-TEST

The scenarios are designed to explore a plausible future for the organization so the organization can be better prepared to respond should that future happen. Properly thinking through the strategic implications of each scenario is the critical step in making this process a useful and practical one for management teams.

In the fifth step, the scenarios and signposts are presented, discussed, and agreed upon by the important stakeholder group in workshops. Leaders need to be able to step back from the fray and see what meaningful insights can be gleaned from the scenarios that will shape future strategic options and actions.

Strategic choices and strategic options are also identified. The strategic choices are the explicit and implicit choices the organization has made in developing its strategy. They will be rated in the various scenarios to assess the fit within the external environment. The goal is to create a thorough framework to stress-test the strategic options. A clear evaluation framework makes sure strategic options are in line with the company's risk tolerance.

KEY ACTIVITIES AND WORK PRODUCTS

- Issue workshop materials to be read in advance
  - Develop and issue materials for workshop participants to review in advance of workshops to confirm and stress-test scenarios and signposts.

- Discuss and confirm trends and scenarios
  - Now it's important to engage a broad group of stakeholders on the scenarios developed for input and engagement. In part, you want to identify anything the smaller group missed. Also, by doing this you ensure broader approval because people feel they've had some input into the process—it isn't just a top-down management strategy.

- Confirm current strategy
  - Study the current strategy and break the strategy down to strategic choices. (Strategic choices embody the strategic direction of an organization.)
  - Consider these elements: strategy, growth (organic and inorganic), customers, competitors, processes, systems, organization, capabilities, culture, and technology.

- Stress-test the strategic plans
  - In this important step in the scenario planning process, strategic plans are thoroughly stress-tested to assess their robustness and resilience in the event any of the identified scenarios occur.
  - Understand what the implications of each scenario are on each strategy and decision.
  - Explore what each scenario means with regard to the design and timing of each strategy. Taking one scenario at a time, the leadership group should evaluate each scenario against the strategy and define which elements stay the same and which of them change. They should explore the opportunities and threats, as well as strengths and weaknesses, that will be uncovered.
  - Identify any contingency planning needs that might be required. Also consider the strategic flexibility that might be required, as well as elements of business resilience, including portfolio, financial, stakeholder, operational, talent management, and marketing.
  - Identify further business opportunities that the scenario might create for the organization.
  - Identify further signposts, both internal and external, that will require ongoing monitoring as part of each scenario and update those signposts.
  - Develop a strategy for each of your four scenarios. If, for example, one strategy assumes the Democratic party wins a U.S. election and you know it does not support Canadian crude pipelines, that would inform one set of strategies compared to a pro-pipeline Republican party winning the election. Some strategies will change for each scenario, whereas other elements of the strategies will stay the same. (Some elements of a strategy will remain the same; these are called the base factors within the strategies. An example of a base factor might be innovation, since it could be important to all scenarios.)

HELPFUL TOOLS AND ACCELERATORS

Options funnel

Business resilience model

Strategic options matrix

STRATEGIC OPTIONS MATRIX

Strategic options are alternative, action-oriented responses to external circumstances that an organization faces and to which it needs to react and adapt. The strategic options matrix is intended as an easy-to-use, spreadsheet-based, decision-making tool that helps leaders weigh a variety of decisions and choose the best ones to apply to specific situations or problems. It is particularly useful for decisions that require substantial judgment and for which quantitative information may not always be available. The organization's capability is assessed on a scale, and nine potential strategic choices are provided.

KEY QUESTIONS

- Have the scenarios been widely communicated within the organization?
- Are the scenarios understood by the wider stakeholder audience? Do they buy in?
- Does the organization understand the key strategic choices they have to make in each scenario? Have the appropriate options been considered?
- Have specific strategic initiatives and opportunities been identified for each scenario that allow the organization to respond and adapt?
- Does the organization understand the specific timing of strategic choices?

- In some cases, are strategic opportunities (e.g., mergers and acquisitions [M&A]) identified in each scenario and understood by leadership?
- Have strategies that remain the same regardless of the scenario been identified?
- Is it clear from the stress-testing which specific actions and decisions need to be taken by the organization?
- Have a series of potential decisions been selected and dependencies between them identified?
- Are business leaders having the right quality strategic conversations?
- Is there the right leadership capability in the organization for each scenario?
- What has the organization learned from the scenario planning process going back to the original focal question?
- Using each scenario, how would the organization answer the original focal question?
- Can the scenarios be understood by front-line employees?
- What future does the organization want and what steps can be taken to ensure it happens?

6. MONITOR SIGNPOSTS AND EXECUTE STRATEGIES

An organization's strategy should be reviewed periodically to ensure its validity in an ever-changing environment. This can take many forms, including strategies, actions, new relationships, meetings, campaigns, projects, policies, and innovations.

In the sixth step, an "early warning" monitoring system is developed to keep track of changes in the external environment and assess the probability of the scenarios. Regular testing of scenarios improves their effectiveness.

It's important to develop a structured approach to obtain input from experts on key change indicators, report the current assessment of the scenarios, and assess the implications on the organization's strategic options.

KEY ACTIVITIES AND WORK PRODUCTS

- Examine monitoring needs and requirements
  - Monitoring the external environment is vital to managing uncertainty. Monitoring outcomes often includes information on scenario probability, development of key uncertainties, perspectives of internal and external experts, etc.
  - Ensure that internal monitoring needs are also considered so that an organization's performance is understood, including elements of sales related to customers, productivity, output, margins, and other relevant metrics.

- Identify the key change indicators
  - Deduct key change indicators that relate to the identified key uncertainties to predict a particular scenario outcome. These are events, developments, or opinions that inhibit or enable changes in the external environment and are indicative of changes in the key uncertainties.
  - Select a balanced set of indicators that are representative, valid, and significant and that can be measured to provide an estimation on the overall development of the key uncertainties.

- Identify an expert panel
  - Identify an expert panel of subject matter experts to get input on change indicators, scenarios, and impacts on strategic options. They can consist of experts either internal to the organization and/or external to the organization.

- Execute strategies
  - Begin to execute strategies while monitoring the various sign-posts, course correcting the strategy and strategy execution as the environment changes.
  - Continue to adapt and pivot various actions, relationships, meetings, campaigns, projects, policies, and innovations as signposts indicate a particular scenario playing out.

HELPFUL TOOLS AND ACCELERATORS

Balanced scorecard

Implementation process map

BALANCED SCORECARD

Adjusting the company's balanced scorecard in a way that allows for the consideration of future potential scenarios is critical to success. Signpost-related indicators should be integrated into the scorecard for the enterprise. The balanced scorecard approach, developed by Robert Kaplan and David Norton and explained in the *Harvard Business Review*, establishes a formal reporting structure with target audiences for each KPI. It ensures that management reporting focuses on the most important strategic issues and helps companies continue to monitor the execution of the strategy.[10]

- The balanced scorecard includes financial measures that tell the results of actions already taken and complements the financial measures with operational measures. Stakeholders can look at the business from four perspectives:

- Customer perspective (How do customers see us?)
- Internal perspective (What must we, as an organization, excel at?)
- Innovation and learning perspective (How can we continue to improve and create value?)
- Financial perspective (How do shareholders see us?)

KEY QUESTIONS

- Does the organization understand what leading/lagging[11] signposts need to be monitored in the external environment?
- Does the organization understand what leading/lagging signposts needs to be monitored internally?
- Do the signposts allow for the right level of anticipation of external realities?
- Has the organization established frequent monitoring of signposts to report results?
- Has the right escalation path been established that allows for early warnings to occur?
- Is the organization ready to execute strategies, take action, and make decisions based on early warning systems?
- Does the organization fully understand the different types of strategic actions that should be considered and can be taken?
- Are the expert panel properly engaged on a regular basis?

In summary, when applying scenario planning within an organization, it's important to take a methodical and structured approach to developing and implementing the tool. The degree of detail and analysis performed depends on the business and market context and what you hope to achieve. Scenario planning can be easily scaled up or down to fit the needs of the organization.

■ ■ ■

SUMMARY KEY POINTS

- There are six tightly integrated steps involved in scenario planning.
- In the first step of the scenario development process, the project scope and time frame should be defined to ensure the outcomes achieve the intended objectives.
- Exploring the market environment is essential to reveal the elements beneath the visible surface of change. These driving forces can affect the organization to varying degrees.
- Predetermined elements are predictable, while uncertainties and risks are unpredictable. It's important to cast a critical eye toward the external environment and document and analyze what could happen to the organization if these risks and uncertainties occur.
- It is not possible to identify all the forces at play; otherwise, you could perfectly predict the future.
- Visualizing the scenarios makes the scenarios come to life and clearly illustrates the implications of each scenario. Scenarios should be written like a story to engage readers.
- Scenarios and resulting strategies should include both a qualitative description and a quantitative aspect, including financials, models, and other important data points.
- The scenarios should be about exploring a plausible future for the organization, so that it can be better prepared to respond, react, and adapt. Properly thinking through the strategic implications and options of each scenario is the critical step in making this process a useful one for management teams.

- An organization's strategy should be reviewed periodically and measured against the predefined scenarios to ensure its validity in an ever-changing environment.
- Scenarios have a shelf life, therefore it's important to keep them fresh and up to date.

CHAPTER 4

LEVELS OF APPLICATION

"Out of intense complexities, intense simplicities emerge."

—Winston Churchill

In this chapter, we look at how scenario planning is flexible and adaptable in many different situations, from industrial or organizational applications to addressing dramatic international issues, as we'll see in one of the most famous examples, the "Mont Fleur" scenario.

As a child, I lived for two years in Lesotho, a small, independent state within South Africa, where my father, a construction engineer, was building an airport at the capital city of Maseru. It was the mid-1980s, so we were there during the apartheid system of institutionalized racism. As young as I was, that experience resonated with me as I observed and experienced the day-to-day inequities of segregation and the oppression of white rule. We left a few years before anti-apartheid political leader Nelson Mandela was released from prison in February 1990 but when I travelled back to South Africa as a young man, I witnessed a transformation.

At the time of Mandela's release, South Africa was in crisis, a country dealing with violent political unrest, catastrophic social decline, and economic collapse as negotiations to end apartheid took place. From 1991 to 1992, in a novel use of the scenario planning methodology, two dozen prominent South African politicians, academics, activists, and business leaders from across the political spectrum came together at the Mont Fleur conference centre outside Capetown to creatively brainstorm the future of their country.

The four weekend sessions were led by Adam Kahane, who was at the time working for the multinational oil company Royal Dutch Shell, which had pioneered scenario planning. Kahane was head of the company's team that created scenarios for potential economic, political, environmental, and social developments that could affect Shell's corporate strategies. Over the years, Shell's scenario department has helped the company respond quickly to global oil crises, the fall of the Soviet Union, the rise of Islamic radicalism, and growing pressure to improve environmental policies.[1]

The Mont Fleur scenario exercise is considered inspiring because it brought together a disparate group of participants and helped them move past their differences and focus on what they had in common: a commitment to the future of South Africa. It painted a picture of four scenarios, from the worst-to best-case outcomes. The discussions were often difficult, but in the end, scenario planning helped create positive forward momentum at a time when the country had been severely polarized. It managed to remove power and politics from the process.[2]

In 1996, when I returned to South Africa to visit friends and four years later when I returned to do research for my MBA, I observed a transformed country. When Nelson Mandela became president, he could have adopted a policy of revenge and retribution for his 27 years in prison.

Instead, he focused on reconciliation, peace, and forgiveness. A central component of this was the Truth and Reconciliation Commission, established in 1995, that investigated human rights violations and provided an outlet for grievances.

South Africa had become fully democratic, with universal suffrage, and had remained peaceful during this transition. I could feel the excitement as the country took those first steps as the new "Rainbow Nation." One of the first things I noticed, on buses, in restaurants, and everywhere I went, was that all forms of segregation had disappeared. The country was re-entering the larger world: global trade had resumed and there was a sense the country was regaining its status and would become an economic powerhouse. Flights in and out of the country were easier to book, and in 1995 South Africa had hosted the rugby World Cup. As any rugby fan would know, South Africa had been banned from participating until apartheid was abolished, so this was a very big deal for everyone.

Thinking back to the Mont Fleur exercise that helped South Africa along this path, too often scenario planning is assumed to be a tool that applies only to private sector companies. Mont Fleur was an example of its versatility, how it can be successful in big, bold government and public sector applications like South Africa's dismantling of apartheid and its gradual transition toward a more democratic nation. It illustrated how scenario planning is really about helping people think creatively, stretch their mental models, engage with a diverse team, and hopefully prepare themselves to deal with even the most severe challenges.

■ ■ ■

In this chapter we take a deep dive into the many different system and organizational levels to which scenario planning can be applied. It's not exclusively an organizational tool but can be effective with high-level global issues as well as being applied to simple business unit and functional strategies. It is a strategic tool for problems, big or small.

Strategy development and the identification and mitigation of related risks occur at different levels in an organization. At the enterprise level, strategy sets the overall direction of vision, mission, and strategic objectives for the entire organization. Risks at the enterprise level are broader in nature and potential impact and are usually captured as part of an enterprise risk management process and are the responsibility of the chief risk officer. Strategies and risks cascade and translate down within the organization to more specific business units, functional and project-related strategies and risks that are more detailed in nature, which eventually further cascade to individual team performance goals of employees.

Strategy and risk can be all-encompassing at the macro level and more focused and tactical as you dig down into an organization, into specific business units and functions. Yet the application of scenario planning is the same. Scenario planning offers a powerful approach to testing strategies, making complex decisions, enhancing risk management, generating innovative initiatives, building optionality, improving organizational learning, and understanding uncertainty at different levels in the organization. It's just the level of specificity and detail that increases as you probe down into the organization and toward the front-line employees where the work gets done.

Scenario planning can be used at the enterprise and wider global level, but the methodology also lends itself to tackling very specific issues: investment decisions and competitive situations focused on how to introduce new products and services in the market and build new organizational capability, competency, and capability into the future.

Chapter 3 explained the generic process of developing and executing scenarios and, as the first step, to "define the scope and identify major stakeholders." This explained why it's important to agree on the level at which scenario planning will be applied. As a follow-up, this chapter explores the differences between levels of scenario planning, between scenario planning and other planning tools that are modelling-centred or more qualitative, and between scenario planning and forecasting. At each level the inputs, scope, process, and resulting outputs vary, but the overarching objective stays the same. Furthermore, the stakeholders involved change from executive-level leaders at the macro level down to front-line employees within a business unit or, at the micro level, a specific capital project.

SCENARIO PLANNING IS NOT FORECASTING

Scenario planning is focused on the future, and on defining different stories behind different paths that will lead to that future. We could also say it is based on a dynamic sequence of interacting events, based on casual processes and critical decision points.[3] Scenario planning offers enhanced flexibility and preparedness to deal with risk and uncertainty, as opposed to purely quantitative forecasting. It is about understanding multiple plausible futures without blinkers on; about identifying what an organization thinks could happen and describing that outcome in a compelling, engaging narrative. Scenarios are also collaborative—typically involving teams of people, often from various levels—and there is often a creative dimension, as opposed to being purely based on quantitative number-crunching.

Forecasts, on the other hand, are constructed on the assumption that the world in the future looks much like today. Forecasts are less creative, and they do not anticipate major shifts in the business environment, which can cause significant challenges for organizational strategy and a firm's performance. In addition, forecasts do not factor in risks and uncertainty as part of a wider stakeholder dialogue or research exercise. Instead, forecasting uses quantitative inputs and methodology to help predict what will, or should, happen in the future by relying mainly on historical data. Forecasts offer one possible future, whereas scenarios offer multiple possible futures.

Forecasting is a shorter-term tool that provides certainty based on some known variables in the system (e.g., passenger traffic for airlines) whereas scenarios provide longer-term, multiple futures based on unknown risks and uncertainties (e.g., the results of a U.S. election). Neither tool is better than the other; they simply offer different approaches to solving different problems that the organization faces and should be used in a complementary way.

Table 1 provides a more detailed contrast between scenario planning and forecasting, comparing various features and an explanation of the differences.

KEY QUESTIONS

- Is the future uncertain and unpredictable or certain and predictable?
- Are one or multiple futures more likely?
- Is the focus on qualitative or quantitative analysis?
- Is the organization looking for an objective, fact-based discussion with stakeholders or a subjective, wider-ranging discussion?
- Is the organization looking for a shorter-term (within one year) or longer-term (multi-year) perspective on the future?
- Can the results from the analysis be replicated on an ongoing basis or are they a one-time, unique representation of information?

TABLE 1

Comparison of Forecasting and Scenario Planning

	FORECASTING	SCENARIO PLANNING
Purpose	• Prediction of the future based on past historical information • Planning for one future	• Thinking process to consider potential futures based on risks and uncertainties • Planning for multiple futures
Certainty	• Probable	• Plausible
Information Type	• Quantitative	• Qualitative and quantitative
Risks and Uncertainties	• Does not factor in risks and uncertainties, more about certainty	• Considers risks and uncertainties
Testing	• Can be tested for accuracy	• Difficult to test for accuracy
Theoretical Basis	• Based on a theoretical model • Future can be predicted	• Based on relationships and causality • Future is unpredictable
Stakeholder Engagement	• Narrow set of stakeholders involved in the process	• Wide set of stakeholders involved in the process from across the organization, internal and sometimes external
Objectivity	• Objective—fact based	• Subjective—guessing and assumptions
Accountability	• Expert analysts, financial planners	• CEO, top-level executives, chief strategy officer, facilitators, consultants, scenario planners, and strategic planners
Frequency	• Used daily	• Used every 2 to 3 years
Horizon	• Short-term perspective	• Long-term perspective
Repeatability	• Results can be replicated	• Involves unique representations

DIFFERENT LEVELS OF APPLICATION

When applying scenario planning in different contexts, the level of application can vary depending on the specific needs of the organization, leaders, and stakeholders involved. Furthermore, scenarios at different levels can be complementary.[4] Organizations that start at the macro level can later drop down to the industry, enterprise, or organizational level, gaining increasing levels of specificity, detail, and analysis. This helps an organization gain perspective on wider strategic problems or focus more narrowly on very specific problems, such as a particular risk or a new product, service, or capital project.

It's important to remember that organizations are multi-level systems, with information and knowledge flowing both up and down; the organizational learning process is different at different levels.[5] Scenario planning typically happens at the enterprise and organizational levels, with top management taking responsibility, but according to organizational theorist and associate professor Russell Korte, effective scenario planning must cascade down and affect all levels of an organization. Ultimately, you need implementation at all levels to get the full value. By viewing organizations as multi-level systems, leaders can drive enhanced outcomes and performance at every level.

To implement strategies influenced by scenario planning, organizations must understand how learning and information are shared at different levels, and scenario planners need to understand how the linkages at different levels work to ensure the interfaces communicate and integrate.

Another way to think about the different levels of scenario planning is whether they are vision- or decision-driven. Vision-driven scenarios help leaders think unconventionally, question assumptions about the future, help develop strategic options, support organizational learning about the external world, and are not linked to a specific decision or project.[6] Decision-driven scenarios, on the other hand, are more about helping understand the effects of different choices, such as a new service or product, and critically analyzing the options.

To summarize, success is about understanding clearly when and how to apply scenario planning at different levels of an organization, who to involve, and how to integrate and communicate at the different levels.

Outlined in this section is an extensive explanation of the different levels with descriptions of how scenario planning can be successfully applied.

1. MACRO LEVEL

Scenario planning at the macro level tends to be vision-driven, typically involving more than one organization and industry and combining both external and internal factors to create one overarching picture. Global and macro scenarios help with strategic policy, government relations, disease control, emergency management, natural disasters, and cross-sector and military strategies, sometimes involving war. For example, when strategist Herman Khan was at the U.S. RAND Corporation in the 1950s and 1960s, he used scenarios to analyze the potential consequences of a nuclear war between the United States and the U.S.S.R. His approach was broad and macro in nature, its impact affecting a multitude of stakeholders.

Scenarios can be developed for entire countries or for broad issues such as the future of crime or the future of women in society and business. At this macro level, scenarios tend to focus on changes that are outside the scope of Porter's Five Forces; they are more all-encompassing from a political, economic, social, or technological perspective. At the macro level, there is usually greater ambiguity and more unknowns, and it is more difficult to identify the possible futures given the magnitude of complexity, risk, and uncertainty involved.

A further interesting application of scenario planning at the macro political level relates to the U.S. election in November 2020. During the 2020 primary race, the National Task Force on Election Crises, a bipartisan group of worst-case-scenario planners mostly made up of Democrats and anti-Trump Republicans and representing experts in election administration, national security, voting and civil rights, technology, public health, and emergency response, gamed out how to respond strategically to various doomsday options for the approaching election, according to articles by Reid Epstein in the *New York Times*.[7] The task force was dedicated to envisioning and presenting plans for scenarios that could potentially disrupt the election. Epstein reported that the task force began with 65 possibilities before narrowing the list to eight potential calamities, including natural disasters, a successful foreign hack of voting machines, a major candidate challenging the legitimacy of the election and seeking to delegitimize the results, and a president who refuses to participate in a peaceful transfer of power. (Does this sound familiar?) So macro-level scenario planning can be shorter term as well as long term.

From a timeline perspective at the macro level, the horizon might be as long as 20 years or more and focused on broader macro issues, like geopolitics, and macro drivers stimulating broader dialogue on economic, social, technological, and related issues. There is a focus on using tools like PESTEL that lend themselves to more external, as opposed to internal, factors. (Recall that PESTEL stands for political, economic, social, technological, environmental, and legal.)

Successful scenario planning involves a combination of convergent and divergent thinking. Convergent thinking is a term defined by Joy Paul Guilford, an American psychologist, as the ability to give the "correct" answer to standard questions that do not require significant innovation or an aligned solution. It focuses on finding a concrete solution to a problem. Divergent thinking refers to opening the mind in various directions, in a spontaneous and nonlinear way, and exploring multiple solutions to a problem. Organizations need patience to stay with the creative, sometimes uncomfortable and confusing divergent thinking phase long enough to get the ideas on the table, followed by the conviction to move on to the convergent thinking phase.[8]

Recent events caused by the global COVID-19 pandemic provide a very real example of the application of scenario planning at the macro level, but perhaps with a shorter time frame than we would normally see. For example, once control measures had been put in place, researchers in China used scenario planning to help model the first and second waves of the virus after considering aspects of transmissibility and severity outside Hubei.[9] Meanwhile, governments and organizations all over the world looked for ways to plan for the future based on possible contagion impacts and different scenarios on how long the virus will sustain itself. The Atlanta-based Centers for Disease Control and Prevention (CDC) developed five COVID-19 pandemic planning scenarios designed to help inform decisions by modellers and public health officials. They were used to evaluate the potential effects of different community migration strategies and help hospitals assess resource needs when the pandemic surged.[10]

Another source of concern is the rise of global warming, with the prevalence of flooding in many coastal regions presenting an ever-increasing risk to millions of people. Three researchers, Mei-Shiang Chang, Ya-Ling Tseng, and Jing-Wen Chen, used scenario planning to create a decision-making tool for government agencies to use in planning for emergency flood logistics.[11] The scenario planning approach developed by these researchers allowed for determination of a resource distribution system for urban flood disasters, covering the structure of rescue organizations, locations and distribution of rescue resources, and the allocation of resources under capacity restrictions. By using data processing and network analysis of a geographic information system, scenario planning helped estimate potential flood locations, pinpoint rescue points, and calculate the required amounts of equipment needed.

A further interesting example at the macro level is the application of scenario planning to broader conservation challenges. Scenario planning provides a framework for establishing more resilient conservation policies in an uncertain world faced with pressures from growing populations and climate change. It also provides increased understanding of key uncertainties, alternative perspectives on conservation planning, and a greater understanding of the consequence of decisions.[12]

KEY QUESTIONS

- Is the focus on understanding global macro-level risks and uncertainties?
- Is there a high level of ambiguity involved in the macro system being assessed?
- Is the planning horizon 20 years or more?
- Is the impact broader than a specific organization or industry?
- Does knowledge transfer need to occur between sectors and organizations within each sector?
- Are the risks and uncertainties far-reaching, such as technological advances, climate change, disease, and natural disasters?

CASE STUDY
Royal Society of Chemistry (Engaging the Community in Organizational Learning)

The Royal Society of Chemistry (RSC) is a professional association whose goal is to "advance excellence in the chemical sciences for the benefit of science and humanity." RSC has over 54,000 members and is headquartered in London, England. The organization carries out research, publishes journals, and hosts conferences and other gatherings. The professional body also rewards certifications and fellowships.

WHY AND HOW SCENARIO PLANNING WAS USED

RSC's goal was not only to envision the future for the organization but also "to understand how the chemical sciences might evolve over the next 10 to 20 years, and how the changes might impact industry, academia, and society at large." Near the end of 2014, RSC began a long-range planning initiative to identify possible future trends for chemical sciences and to plan and prepare for them.

RSC's leadership team began by identifying high-level focus questions to be answered, such as "If public funding is not available to support the type of blue-skies research that has traditionally produced the next major advances, how will future research be funded?" RSC established a one-day workshop for its leadership team to begin a process of answering these questions in the form of scenarios. The approach consisted of three phases:

1. For three months, over 50 stakeholders from industry, government, and academia were interviewed to identify possible trends.

2. Follow-ups were performed with stakeholders in order to understand controversial viewpoints and secure engagement by industry leaders.

3. Three one-day scenario planning workshops (in the United Kingdom and United States) were run to identify weak signals and emerging catalysts for future change; they evolved into four scenarios.

ORGANIZATIONAL BENEFITS AND RESULTS

RSC's chief executive, Robert Parker, announced the scenario planning process as "the beginning of a conversation with our community" to assist its organization (along with the wider stakeholder community) in organizational learning about the future of science. The report was shared to develop community relations, and the leadership set a new goal of improving dialogue with its broader community, given the importance of stakeholder relations.

In addition, RSC has used scenario planning to more clearly advocate for investments and programs by outlining what tomorrow may look like for the field. Based on the scenarios, RSC launched new activities, such as advancing scholarly communication by open-access publishing. During various scenario planning workshops, RSC monitored for important signals to help it better understand important trends, such as an increasing public interest in science, and then used this information to help develop scenarios. The benefit of this exercise was to ensure validity and reliability of scenarios by grounding them in current data.

RSC's current acting chief executive has expressed interest in returning to scenario planning as COVID-19 continues to alter the global landscape.[13]

2. INDUSTRY LEVEL

At the industry level, the focus of scenario planning is on broad challenges like oil prices, trade, sustainability issues, alliances, policy strategies, and other macro factors that impact a specific industry or segment of the market. It's about the environment and the transfer of knowledge between organizations in a single sector, joint ventures, partnerships, and cross-selling. Industry-level scenario planning also requires divergent thinking in order to generate cross-industry innovations, strategies, and thinking beyond the confines of business-as-usual.

When performing scenario planning at the industry level, it's important not to draw the boundaries too narrowly, according to Russell Korte, but to think broadly and, in some cases, bring in ideas, risks, and uncertainties from the outside. It's also about relationships between organizations and competitive dynamics within the industry.[14]

There are several examples of real-life applications of scenario planning at this level. For example, in the U.K. textiles and clothing industry, scenario planning was used to help understand the sustainability of the industry in the long term, given the competition from lower-cost markets like China, and to understand the broader sustainability of the industry, including aspects of the triple bottom line. Scenario planning was applied to the entire sector to help evaluate the trade-offs between economic, environmental, and social impacts in the United Kingdom to help anticipate outcomes.[15]

A further example of industry-level scenario planning is the airline industry in Europe, known to be highly competitive among long-time, well-established organizations like British Airways, KLM, and Air France, and the more recent low-cost carriers like easyJet and Ryanair. Researchers in Europe explored the use of scenario planning and the design of a knowledge-based system in strategic decision-making in the context of the European airline industry.[16] As a result of this research, strategic decisions taken by leaders became more effective (coupled with the application of AI).

In the government and public sector, scenario planning is widely used in urban regional transit planning, with an example in Houston, where it was applied to support practical transportation and urban planning needs.[17, 18] The Virginia Transportation Research Council also used scenario-based transportation planning to help evaluate different policy scenarios, an undertaking that is typical of many planning authorities around the world.[19]

One final example relates to agriculture. In Scotland, scenario planning was used to help assess the future of the sheep and cattle industries relating to their resilience to disease. Four scenarios, with different macro forces, were examined as a way to better understand how to make the industries less vulnerable to diseases. Aspects of demographics, government support, regulation, technology, and innovation were considered.[20] In this case, the value of scenario planning was seen as providing a mechanism for dialogue and knowledge-sharing among the stakeholders within the farming community and government, and informing future disease contingency plans.

Both the macro- and industry-level scenario planning tend to heavily rely on aspects of PESTEL during the exploration of the environment phase of the process. This particular tool lends itself well to external trends, risks, uncertainties, and analysis, and ensures all potential driving forces are considered.

KEY QUESTIONS

- Does the transfer of knowledge need to occur among organizations within a sector?

- Do the risks and uncertainties relate to policy-related industry strategies?
- Is the planning horizon 10 years or more?
- Are strategic alliances and partnerships among organizations an important consideration as part of the strategic process?
- Is the sector or industry at large facing considerable external challenges and pressures?

CASE STUDY
International Atomic Energy Agency (Future Preparation)

The International Atomic Energy Agency (IAEA) is an organization made up of 171 member states that is tasked with advocating for the peaceful use of nuclear energy and assurance that the technology is not being used for military purposes, such as an atomic bomb. IAEA is headquartered in Vienna, Austria, but has large offices in Toronto, Canada, and Tokyo, Japan. IAEA's Department of Safeguards is regarded as the world's nuclear inspectorate.

WHY AND HOW SCENARIO PLANNING WAS USED
Historically, IAEA's Department of Safeguards conducted both regular strategic reviews and external environmental analyses as part of its scope, until an outside source recommended scenario planning as a management tool to enhance the strategy process. Along with supporting intradepartmental decision-making, IAEA was interested in being better prepared for the future and addressing the perceived need to consider a wider set of drivers of change given the increasing overall unpredictability about the future.

The department hired experts to provide educational courses, which started with a two-day workshop. The process of scenario planning followed these phases of activity:

1. Preliminary research was conducted, and then small subgroups would draft scenarios together.

2. Common themes were identified from the small subgroup work products, and four scenarios that had various drivers were defined.

3. The scenarios were first presented to the senior leadership and then refined during a two-week process that solicited input from the middle-management participants.

4. Eight months after a strategic review was conducted, new staff members and the senior leaders critiqued the scenarios for "plausibility, relevance, and ability to challenge."

ORGANIZATIONAL BENEFITS AND RESULTS

A critical adaptation was made eight months after the scenarios were first drafted: to provide names for the scenarios so they could be used regularly and easily among staff in conversation—the names helped tell a story. Condensing the scenarios to easily digestible topics empowered the organization to collaborate more freely and to feel comfortable using scenarios.

The department's strategic plans and objectives were directly informed by these scenarios. For instance, one objective was "Leverage and establish partnerships" to assist with future planning. The scenario planning activity was also used in order to highlight blind spots in the departments' analyses. One of the scenarios asked "What would the nuclear industry look like in 2030?", and in the team's analysis, transportable reactors were mentioned as a possible innovation idea. As a result, the department began planning and innovating for the type of safeguard approaches needed for these potential reactors.

As a consequence of scenario planning, the department has moved to a "living" strategic plan, which has increased the organization's agility and nimbleness to respond to the future.[21, 22]

3. ORGANIZATION / ENTERPRISE LEVEL

Organization-or enterprise-level scenario planning is perhaps the most popular, with established examples at organizations like Shell, British Telecom, and GE. This level of scenario planning is focused on wider strategic issues that face the organization as well as a cross-section of strategic investment decisions that need to be made. Risks and uncertainties at this level are still strategic and external, and the planning horizon can still be longer term in nature. Within an organization, there are many different levels of analysis that can be performed, from a global and externally focused one to digging down into the guts of an organization, focusing on complex internal issues. These external uncertainties and internal complexities need to come together as crucial inputs when performing organization-wide scenario planning.

One way of thinking about organization-level scenario planning is in terms of Porter's Five Forces, which we looked at in an earlier chapter. It is an effective way of analyzing an organization's competitive environment: the number and power of an organization's competitive rivals, potential new market entrants, suppliers, customers, and substitute products that can influence performance—these should all be considered as part of the scenario planning process at this level. In addition, external analysis using

PESTEL should not be ignored; it is of great use when doing macro- or industry-level scenario planning. It's important to remember, though, that while external factors are part of the process, they are not the sole focus. A careful balance of internal complexity and external risk and uncertainty should be considered.

Scenario planning at this level is also about how an organization formulates a competitive differentiation and strategy and looks at what is happening within an industry. Understanding the behaviour of competitors—for example, where they are investing and how the internal portfolio is balanced against others to deal with the risks and uncertainties—helps drive competitive advantage. At this level, the planning process tends to focus on micro-industry factors, narrow external forces, and a mix of long- and short-term factors but still includes a proper study of risks and uncertainty. It's about ensuring the strategy is properly validated and tested for long-term success. It also supports a company in properly assessing complex decisions that have organization-wide impacts.

At the organizational level, a range of possible futures are considered—typically three to five scenarios—and understanding the implications of each one for the organization is critical to success. It's common that probabilities cannot be defined for each scenario, making it more about core strategies, competencies, and capabilities within the organization, as well as relationships, routines, practices, and culture. Furthermore, scenario planning identifies necessary structural and process-related changes an organization needs to make in the future. From a strategy-testing and validation perspective, the foundational strategy usually remains unchanged, regardless of the scenario defined. An example might be an automotive company that, regardless of scenarios, will always sell cars, its core business. But if a scenario revealed that a government initiative will introduce new emissions regulations, that policy might trigger a specific strategy relating to an investment in innovations to reduce emissions.

Finally, just like at macro and industry levels, organizational scenario planning requires a combination of divergent and convergent thinking. Organizations need to broadly explore ideas and possibilities for the future, but also get specific and narrow on how the organization will react in each case, should they happen.

KEY QUESTIONS

- Is a combination of strategic visioning and complex decision-making required?
- Is the transfer of knowledge solely within the organization?
- Are a combination of macro and micro factors and drivers considered?
- Is there a combination of multiple futures?
- Is there a combination of broad external and narrow internal complexities, risks, and uncertainties considered?
- Is the planning horizon 5 to 10 years?

4. BUSINESS-UNIT / FUNCTIONAL LEVEL

There is lots of literature on the application of scenario planning at the organizational, or enterprise, level, but limited information at the business unit, or functional, level.

One study of interest looked at the business unit of the U.K. division of a leading multinational enterprise specializing in beauty and cosmetic products.[23] When scenario planning was applied at the business-unit level, the results showed that the organization was less likely to distinguish between risks and uncertainties, it lacked planning horizons, and internal uncertainties tended to be business unit–specific. In addition, scenarios were more focused on internal factors and resource analysis as a source of competitive advantage.

At the business-unit level, scenarios are more aligned to the investment decisions and specific strategic issues related to the company's products or services. Scenario planning at this level requires convergent thinking and tends to focus on decisions to make in the short term. Uncertainties are more operational in nature and tough to separate from risks; the planning horizon is shorter and uncertainties are more internal in focus.

In multinational organizations with operations around the world, these types of scenarios can also relate to a specific country and the dynamics within that country, similar to a business unit. Issues facing multinationals at the country level tend to be specific, nuanced, and characterized by economics or politics at that time. So some level of external analysis can be involved, depending on the size and complexity of the company.

In addition, the focus at this level deals with the complexity of internal issues. For a range of futures that are mutually exclusive and collectively exhaustive, a firm can develop implications, assign probabilities to each outcome, assign the dynamic path to each outcome, assess payoffs of each strategic option in each scenario, assess how each strategic option might influence probability, and make an eventual decision. Probabilities can usually be defined at the business-unit or functional level, since the information gathered is quantitative in nature.

Different business units and functions focus on different elements of the results from organization-level scenario planning and will take different results forward. From this information, a firm can produce different interpretations relevant to the business unit or function, but overall alignment to the enterprise planning process is still important.

KEY QUESTIONS

- Is the focus on translating organizational or enterprise-wide scenarios into specific business unit or function scenarios?
- Do specific decisions need to be made based on the assessment of various future options?
- Is the focus on maximizing existing products and services within a business unit?
- Are price, cost, supply, and demand involved in the process?
- Is more financial information involved in the decision-making process?

5. PROJECT LEVEL

This level of scenario planning considers the specifics around a major investment strategy and, in many ways, is similar to business-unit and functional planning. For example, Shell used scenario planning in the context of some of its major LNG and deep-water capital projects that involved multi-billion-dollar investment decisions and combined scenario planning with investment option tools (like real option analysis) to make important strategic decisions. Scenario planning helps Shell with project analysis by identifying future project options and the timing of decisions and provides important input to help evaluate project options.[24] Project-specific scenario planning typically considers prices, margins, project risks, and options on technical design and execution strategies.

At the project level, the future is more predictable, making it easier to choose the strategic investment decision best suited to a range of outcomes; financial information plays a very important role in the process of making the decision. Capital projects can be very large (sometimes billions of dollars), involve thousands of people, and have a make-or-break impact on the company, so properly considering future realities, using scenario planning tools, helps deal with this complexity.

KEY QUESTIONS

- Is the focus on making a specific investment decision related to a capital project?
- Do different project options exist?
- Is the project complexity large and one that can have considerable negative or positive impacts on the organization overall?
- Is the decision-making process purely internal in nature?
- Are there a range of technical considerations to factor in?

CASE STUDY

National Health Service (Using Scenario Planning to Drive Initiative Implementation)

The National Health Service (NHS) is a component of the United Kingdom's Department of Health, which administers health care to the general public. This case study focuses on NHS's GS1 Healthcare User Group (HUG), which was established in 2009 to drive the adoption of radio frequency identification (RFID) across the health care system.

WHY AND HOW SCENARIO PLANNING WAS USED

HUG was an organization-wide project focused on "promoting RFID in operational areas of NHS, where the benefits of adopting the technology had been proven, but not implemented." HUG did not have the funding to direct change but rather helped shape and orchestrate developments and system-wide learning. Thus HUG was eager to engage health care professionals and convince them of the long-term benefits of adding RFIDs as a way to increase information and technological capabilities. The group wanted to develop a scenario-driven road-mapping process, so it ran a project that lasted 16 days and involved various stages of activity, as follows:

1. In the first stage, participants of the primary workshop were asked questions that highlighted issues relating to the current methods being used to illustrate how RFID could be used instead.

2. For the second stage, interviews were conducted and 37 driving forces were identified across a PESTEL analysis, with each participant ranking driving forces by importance and uncertainty.

3. And lastly, a series of workshops were conducted to facilitate a deductive approach to building the scenarios. Five 2-by-2 matrices were built in the workshops, corresponding to 20 different scenarios.

ORGANIZATIONAL BENEFITS AND RESULTS

The team at HUG noticed that at first people involved in the project were reluctant to consider 15 years into the future. They were comfortable with a shorter period, say one to three years. However, once driving forces were identified it became much clearer to participants the reason for long-term planning as a way of dealing with these challenging long-term uncertainties. This was a clear example of how HUG fostered *organizational learning* among the health care professionals engaged in the workshops, as line-duty workers began to see the advantage of preparing for the longer-term future.

NHS also identified *"flex points" (similar to signposts)*, which were significant changes or events in the present as well as over the next 15 years. These originated from participants considering

"What would need to happen for each scenario to take place?" When HUG's team engaged people in considering options for the future, it sparked a conversation about how they might begin planning for the next phase of health care.[25]

6. INDIVIDUAL / JOB PERFORMANCE LEVEL

The final, and perhaps most informal, level of scenario planning is at the individual, or job performance, level. It's here that employees tackling day-to-day issues might consider possible future realities as they execute their own work. At this level, risk, uncertainty, and complexity tend to be more manageable and have clear forecasts, and it's more likely it will be possible to model the impact of uncertainty through sensitivity analysis. The nature of sensitivity analysis tends to be operational and financial in nature, internally focused rather than strategic.

A further consideration at the individual and performance level is translating scenarios performed at the organization, enterprise, business-unit, or functional level. For strategies resulting from the scenario planning process to be properly executed and implemented, translation, communication, and integration need to occur, starting at the top of the organization and filtering down to the front line, so their usefulness for the individual is understood. These individuals will use their own perceptions and filters, so organizations need to clearly provide them with the learning outcome.

Adam Kahane talks about the "inner game" of transformative scenario planning whereby the wider team generates forward movement but isn't concerned with transforming the system. To succeed at that, it's less important that leaders explore scenarios and make strategic decisions than that they convince employees, from the bottom up, to buy into the strategy.

KEY QUESTIONS

- Is the focus on driving individual performance and behaviour?
- Are you trying to align the organization with the scenario planning outcomes?
- Have you considered how the results of wider organizational scenario planning activities are translated and cascade down to front-line employees?
- Have strategic initiatives that were identified through wider organization-level scenario planning been communicated and assigned to individuals or departments for execution?

In summary, you need to allow leaders to choose the appropriate tools for the problems they are trying to solve.[26] The level of scenario planning in part depends on the level of risk and uncertainty involved as well as the organizational level under consideration. Leaders need to classify the strategic problem they are trying to solve: is this a macro-level economic or societal problem, industry- or organization-focused, or focused more narrowly on a specific business-unit, functional, or project problem? Although the technique for scenario planning is flexible enough to accommodate many different needs, aspects of the process need to be tailored depending on the level at which leaders are operating within the organizational system.

Table 2 provides a summary of the different levels of scenario planning with regard to purpose, scope, mental models, inputs, how risk and uncertainty are considered, focus, timeline, and expertise required to be successful.

TABLE 2
Levels of Scenario Planning Compared

	Macro	Industry	Enterprise	Business Unit, Function, Project, Individual Job
Purpose	• Strategic visioning • Shared sense of possible futures • Transfer of knowledge between organizations in different industries • Learning	• Strategic visioning • Shared sense of possible futures • Transfer of knowledge between organizations in the same industry • Learning	• Strategic visioning / Decision-making • New strategic ideas against possible futures • Transfer of knowledge within the organization • Learning / Strategic choices	• Decision-making and investment management • Test options and understand implications of each option • Align within on the best course of action to solve an issue • Strategic choice when the best option is not obvious
Scope	• Environment, trends, and macro economic forces • Global, broad perspective • Strategic • Cannot define probabilities	• Industry trends, policy and macro economic forces • Industry, broad perspective • Strategic • Cannot define probabilities	• Industry trends, policy, macro economic and micro forces • Company, new products and services, broad and core competencies • Strategic and financial (structural and process changes) • Mixed probabilities	• Micro (specific issues and value chain) • Existing products and services, specific organizational capability • Financial • Probabilities
Mental Models	• Divergent thinking	• Divergent thinking	• Divergent / Convergent thinking	• Convergent thinking
Prevalent Inputs	• PESTEL analysis	• PESTEL analysis	• PESTEL analysis • Porter's Five Forces	• Cost, demand, and price • Data and analytics

TABLE 2
Levels of Scenario Planning Compared *Continued*

	Macro	Industry	Enterprise	Business Unit, Function, Project, Individual Job
Risks and Uncertainties	• High level of ambiguity • Risk understanding • Risks and Uncertainties separated • Broad risks	• Range of futures • Policy alignment • Risks and Uncertainties separated • Broad risks	• Multiple futures • Stress-tested competitive strategy • Risks and Uncertainties separated • Broad and company-specific risks and company complexity	• One future • Investment decision • Risks and Uncertainties combined related to a specific decision • Business-unit, function- and project-specific risks and complexity
Focus	• External	• External	• External and Internal	• Internal
Timeline	• Long term • 20 years +	• Long term • 10 years +	• Long or medium term • 5 to 10 years	• Short term • 1 year
Expertise	• Outside	• Outside/ Inside	• Outside/ Inside	• Inside
Example	• Polar event, climate change, disease control, natural disaster	• Strategic alliance and industry alignment, major sector disruption	• Expand to international markets, mergers and acquisitions, technology change	• New product or service line within a business unit, capital project options

DIFFERENT TYPES OF APPLICATION

In addition to the different levels of application, there are also various approaches to scenario planning itself that can be applied at different levels within an organization.[27] These tend to be related to the approach and focus of the scenario planning exercise and the emphasis placed on the type of analysis involved.

Intuitive logic, for example, is focused on strategically analyzing key decisions and is external in focus (environmental), and many of the variables involved tend to be qualitative in nature. The process itself involves ordering perceptions of alternative futures, with the scenarios representing a unique combination of forces or macro drivers. This approach is very intuitive and logical, relying on the reputation and communication skills of the team involved in the process. It also offers analysis of the implications of each scenario on the organization and lends itself well to macro-, industry-, and, to some extent, organization-level scenario planning.

Trend impact analysis is another type of scenario planning that provides an independent forecast of a dependent variable. It combines traditional forecasting, such as time series analysis and econometrics, with qualitative factors to evaluate probability of occurrence and importance. This method does not evaluate the potential impacts events might have on each other; it is designed for one key decision or forecast variable that is quantitative. It is focused on understanding the probability of events occurring over time and lends itself well to the business-unit/functional approach, or project-level scenario planning.

Cross-impact analysis, the final type of scenario planning approach, helps with forecasting events that are related. It generates scenarios one year at a time, combines the strengths of trend-impact analysis and cross-impact analysis, and produces scenarios that unfold over a longer period and can be interactively modified by the user.

FLEXIBILITY OF SCENARIOS

In summary, the benefit of different scenario planning techniques and their applications is that they are very flexible and can be adapted based on context. Organizations can choose, for example, to simply use one at the organizational level to stress-test a strategy, ensure a broad consideration of risks and uncertainties, and stop there. By contrast, in large multinationals with operations in many different countries or producing multiple products and service lines, organizations can choose a more integrated and cascaded approach where the results from the broad, macro, external organizational exercise can be translated down to the narrower, micro, and internal business unit or project.

In addition, the approach and emphasis of scenario planning can be tailored to the specific needs of an organization, with some electing to include specific quantitative financial modelling under each scenario, while others decide to be purely qualitative in nature. The point is, there is no right or wrong answer, but a context in which each organization exists, facing unique risks and uncertainties that need to be managed, and requiring strategies that need to be formulated and tested so that decisions on major investments can be made. If scenario planning helps optimize success at different levels, then it should be applied.

■ ■ ■

SUMMARY KEY POINTS

- Forecasting is about prediction of the future based on past historical information and planning for the future, whereas scenario planning is more of a thinking process to consider potential futures based on risks and uncertainties and, in turn, planning for various futures.
- Scenario planning can be applied at different levels within the organizational system.
- Vision-driven scenarios help leaders think creatively, question assumptions about the future, develop strategic options, and support organizational learning about the external world not linked to a specific decision or project

- Decision-driven scenarios are more about a specific strategic choice and helping leaders understand the impacts of different choices, such as a new service or product.
- Macro scenario planning tends to be focused on global issues of strategic importance and considers external risks and uncertainties that cross sector boundaries. Divergent thinking is required, involves a high level of ambiguity as it considers the long term (20 years-plus), and typically requires external expertise.
- Industry-level scenario planning is also external in focus but targeted toward industry-specific risks and uncertainties. It involves strategic policy issues, using divergent thinking, considering industry alignment, and looking at a range of possible futures and the transfer of knowledge between organizations.
- Organizational and enterprise-level scenario planning is about strategic visioning but also making cross-enterprise strategic decisions. It's about stress-testing and validating the overall strategy for the organization and supporting complex decision-making and wider organizational learning. Risks and uncertainties, both internal and external, are considered.
- Business-unit or functional level scenario planning occurs within the organization, tends to be internal in focus, requires convergent thinking, is short term, and is focused on how to adjust existing products or services to meet business demands and deal with complexity.
- Project-level scenario planning focuses on considering options on investment decisions. Typically, risks and uncertainties are combined, and probabilities are an important feature.
- Individual and job performance–level scenario planning emphasizes the importance of acting on the results of wider organization-level scenario planning, such as the implementation of strategic initiatives.

- Scenario planning as a management tool offers a lot of flexibility with regard to how, and at what level, it is applied within a system and an organization, and is context specific.

CHAPTER 5

THE EIGHT BENEFITS OF SCENARIO PLANNING

"Foresight is not about predicting the future, it's about minimizing surprise."

—KARL SCHROEDER, AUTHOR AND FUTURIST

After the horror of the September 11, 2001, terrorist attack on the United States, it was obvious that few organizations, public or private, were prepared for an incident like this or how to handle the fallout from its aftermath. One exception was the U.S. Coast Guard, which, in 1998, had begun a scenario planning exercise called "Long View." The organization understood that, in the wake of the collapse of the Soviet Union, the rise of globalization, and the rapid growth of the digital Information Age, the Coast Guard not only needed to continue its long history of swiftly *responding* to events but also needed to better *anticipate* potential future ones. So it introduced a long-range scenario planning exercise to help the organization identify, in real time, potential threats. As a result, the Coast Guard was singled out, above all other U.S. federal services, for its "agility and preparedness" in its response to 9/11.[1]

The Coast Guard example illustrates an extreme benefit of scenario planning—helping a military service deal with life-or-death situations—but the practice provides benefits for many kinds of public and private organizations. In previous chapters, we introduced the definition of scenario planning and explained what it is and how it evolved through history. Next we looked at the challenge of uncertainty and complexity and how scenario planning helps mitigate these external macro forces by providing a more methodical way of understanding and assessing them. The methodology of applying scenario planning in a practical and fit-for-purpose way was analyzed, as well as how scenarios can be used at different levels within an organization or system. This chapter focuses on the many benefits scenario planning offers an organization if executed correctly and illustrates how some of these benefits are interrelated to each other in different ways as either inputs, process, or outputs. In addition, the relative importance of the different benefit components and subcomponents is explained and, finally, a new benefit model is proposed and explained. The benefit model will help organizations rethink the importance of scenario planning and encourage their leaders to take it more seriously.

At a high level, the benefits of scenario planning include the following:

- The ability to stress-test and validate a strategy
- A way to support more complex decision-making
- An expansion of educational (organizational) learning
- A way to become nimbler in response to challenges and opportunities
- The ability to assess uncertainty
- The development of better risk management protocols
- The development of innovative initiatives
- A way to consider a wider array of strategic options

All are important when considering the future direction of an organization, but it's critical to understand what the organization is trying to achieve and what it hopes to get out of the process, because only then will it achieve its objectives and ultimate performance outcomes.

1. STRATEGY VALIDATION AND TESTING

In his 2013 book, *Playing to Win: How Strategy Really Works,* Roger Martin talked about how strategy is an organization's approach to achieving its overall goals—it represents where the organization will play in the market and how the organization will win. It outlines a course of action the organization will take over a period of several years to achieve a vision, mission, or strategic objective. The process of strategy validation and testing is about answering questions such as these: *Do I have it right? What are my gaps? What am I missing?*

Strategy validation and testing can be executed in many ways, including speaking with customers, suppliers, employees, shareholders, partners, and other stakeholders to collect valuable feedback on the strategy. (This is a form of testing to understand what is missing.) Validating and testing a strategy can also involve "piloting," testing a product or service within a specific geographic market, or with a specific customer segment, to gauge the results before undertaking a much wider and riskier mass rollout. Scenario planning is a further example of a method that helps stress-test and validate a strategy to ensure it is versatile, flexible, feasible (that is, *can it successfully be implemented?*), transparent, and robust against different external contexts that could play out. There is no use having a strategy that won't work once implemented and executed. Organizations are always looking for ways to evaluate how competitive their assets are and whether they have the right core capabilities.

In the United States, the Federal Reserve Board (FRB) releases hypothetical scenarios for what it calls stress-testing exercises, which ensure that banks have adequate capital and processes that allow them to continue to lend to businesses and households. The FRB's stress-test framework consists of the Comprehensive Capital Analysis and Review (CCAR) and the Dodd-Frank Act, both of which are used to assess the 34 large banks with more than $100 billion in total assets; each bank is expected to run stress tests against two defined scenarios, including one called "adverse" and another called "severely adverse."[2]

Strategy validation and testing is a way of helping executives learn and have objective discussions about a strategy to evaluate its strengths, weaknesses, and overall resilience. On portfolio management, in particular, it helps leaders understand where the portfolio might have limitations and where acquisitions or divestments might be required. It removes the politics from the process and prevents the executive team from battling for resources, power, and position. The strategy is considered based on what it is, and not on some random preference or gut feeling. It also forces a discussion on a wider set of factors. Planners have a habit of focusing on the most likely future assumptions but scenario planning, with its multiple scenarios, forces everyone to take into account the worst, as well as best-case, possibilities. Furthermore, it prevents individual business units from putting forward cases that benefit their business and the thinking within their silos.

Scenarios help stress-test the viability of current strategies by putting them into a kind of "wind-tunnel" that is used to validate their resilience, resulting in something that is robust and future-proofed. A more precise description, shared by a leader at a large oil and gas company, is that scenario planning is about "stress-testing the strategy until it is internally consistent and plausible in future worlds." Perhaps the most famous example of this practice was that of Royal Dutch Shell, which used scenarios to stress-test its strategy in 1986 to anticipate the drop in oil prices that year with great success.[3]

Strategy validation and testing also questions whether members of management really understand their organization's ability to survive under tough market conditions, as well as which levers can be pulled to manoeuvre into a different, and hopefully more successful, direction. At a more basic level, it can question how things could play out, which horizons leadership should be thinking about, and whether a given strategy will even work. One pipeline executive said, "It helps you question what stays the same with each scenario and what changes strategically."

Scenarios also help inform the specific strategic features of a company. They identify competitive assets and core capabilities and can be used to evaluate the strategies proposed.[4] Similarly, according to planning consultant Paul Schoemaker, scenario planning is important in helping identify what he calls strategic segments in which the firm might be competing, helping delineate the battlefields more clearly.[5]

With regard to iterating, according to Alex Wright, a planning expert at the University of Sheffield, scenario planning can also be thought of as a cyclical approach to strategy incorporating continual monitoring, review, and revision.[6] Wright adds that scenarios are constructed based on the premise that the future cannot be predicted. For that reason, it's important to keep scenarios fresh and up-to-date, or what Wright calls the "quality approach to strategy."

KEY SUB-COMPONENTS OF STRATEGY VALIDATION AND STRESS-TESTING

- Stress and resilience testing
- Competitive asset and core capability identification
- Cyclical and iterative approach to strategy
- Quality management

CASE STUDY
Port of Vancouver (Port 2050: Forming New Partnerships Using Scenario Planning)

The Port of Vancouver is Canada's largest port and the third largest in North American by tons of cargo. It exchanges cargo with more than 170 world economies and is the 44th busiest port in the world. The Port of Vancouver is owned by Vancouver Fraser Port Authority.

WHY AND HOW SCENARIO PLANNING WAS USED

The Port of Vancouver began a scenario planning process in 2010 to "establish a shared vision for the future of the Vancouver Gateway." The initiative was referred to as Port 2050. In 2014, the Port of Vancouver engaged a consultancy firm to design and deliver a program to test the relevancy of the scenarios and to recommend updates. The consultancy firm focused on ensuring a highly collaborative scenario planning process and conducted the following phases:

1. In-depth interviews were undertaken with port leadership, staff, and other experts.

2. A workshop was conducted with over 70 participants to gather input and advice.

3. Draft updates to scenarios and "key drivers of changes" were developed based on interviews, workshop input, and research.

ORGANIZATIONAL BENEFITS AND RESULTS

One of the scenarios, "The Great Transition," was deemed one the port "believes is worth aspiring to." The port defined many of its strategic goals based on this scenario, which outlined a lower carbon economy and a focus on sustainable trade.

By updating its scenario planning process from 2011, the port could make the necessary changes and *adaptations to the strategic plan through testing and validation* to continue forging ahead to 2050.

Based on the 2011 original scenario planning process, the port took strategic action and partnered with BC Hydro in 2013 to focus on one of the scenarios by creating the "Energy Action Initiative" to advance energy conservation and strategic energy planning for port tenants.[7]

2. COMPLEX DECISION-MAKING

Complex decision-making often integrates with strategy validation and testing, because as decisions related to strategy get validated and tested, those decisions can be complex in nature and require considering many different factors. Scenario planning in the context of decision-making is about understanding the known knowns, the known unknowns, and the unknown unknowns. It's also interesting to note the extent to which different CEOs in various companies make decisions based on gut reactions and intuition, which, in a volatile and complex world, does not always end in success. For example, FedEx founder Fred Smith invested $320 million in Zapmail, ultimately a failed experiment. Zapmail, launched in 1984, was a proprietary service offering fax transmissions to customers. But within two years, affordable fax machines that used regular home or business phone lines were available to anyone and FedEx had lost more than $350 million. Today, it is widely accepted that more in-depth research into the company's hunch about the technology, the market, and its customers might have avoided this disaster.[8]

The quality of decision-making is important, and too often companies make decisions without understanding the long-term impact that scenario planning could have identified.

Contrary to the viewpoint that you always need facts and data to make good decisions, Johnson & Johnson CEO Ralph Larsen said that "very often, people will do a brilliant job up through the middle management levels, where it's very heavily quantitative in terms of the decision-making. But then they reach senior management, where the problems get more complex and ambiguous, and we discover that their judgment or intuition is not what it should be."[9]

Perhaps the right answer is a balance between facts, data, and intuition.

Complex decision-making also requires a high degree of collaboration among principal stakeholders, as explained by John Mackey, the CEO of Whole Foods, in an article on the website Big Think Edge in 2017. Mackey explains how he made major decisions at Whole Foods that helped grow the company into a $13.7-billion mega-organization that attracted the attention of Amazon. Mackey said that he "tries to make major decisions at Whole Foods by trying to come to a consensus among the top minds in the company. When disagreements get expressed through the decision-making process," he says, "you generally end up making better decisions." Mackey also noted that "while it takes longer to make the decision, once you begin [to implement it], it goes a lot faster because there isn't the sort of resistance and sabotage that works its way through the organization."

By bringing a variety of stakeholders and perspectives into the complex decision-making process and encouraging those involved to share their different views, the CEO of Whole Foods could identify the issues associated with the direction an initiative had taken and make a better decision as a result. Scenario planning is a highly collaborative process that requires diverse perspectives to support decision-making, and the scenarios themselves represent both ends of the spectrum representing diverse views.

Using scenario planning, realities that could play out are considered, and leaders are encouraged to evaluate the likely consequences rather than make heat-of-the-moment decisions. Scenario planning helps leaders become strategically more prepared to make better decisions. It brings more structure, rigour, and process to the decision-making exercise in a way that ensures a more thoughtful and grounded approach based on facts, data, and information, both internal and external to the organization.

Thomas Chermack, founder and director of the Scenario Planning Institute, outlines the conceptual link between scenario planning and decisions and explains how scenario planning might aid in avoiding decision-making errors on complex processes, especially when something unexpected happens, and how scenario planning can help with both challenges. Furthermore, he proposes that scenario planning decreases "bounded rationality," helps management teams consider internal and external factors, decreases stickiness and friction of information, and expands and provides alternative mental models. The essential idea of scenario planning is to perceive the organization within different external environments and learn from it.[10]

In the model proposed by Chermack, learning in scenario planning is defined as often requiring changes to pre-existing mental models and challenging old assumptions that leaders take for granted and that are deeply rooted. Decisions are made to chart a course of actions and the performance resulting from those actions. Hence, scenarios enable learning, and learning helps change mental models so new and better decisions are made that result in better performance outcomes. Furthermore, change in one unit provokes change in another. Scenarios provoke dialogue, interaction, and thoughtful reflection, and when mental models are adjusted, new insights are revealed and assumptions about the organization and its positioning are changed. Decisions reached through this process are more robust, have considered more options, and have challenged prevailing attitudes.[11]

There is also some evidence that scenario planning might help executives in high-velocity environments make faster decisions. Stanford University's Kathleen Eisenhardt found in her research that faster decision-making was associated with more alternatives or strategic options, which scenario planning helps explore. The research found that comparing alternatives helped decision-makers ascertain the alternative strengths and built confidence in decision-makers. Decision-makers who pursued multiple options became less psychologically trapped and could act better when confronted by negative information.[12]

A further complicating factor is the volume of information that organizational leaders are exposed to in the information age. There is always the concern that the sheer volume of information to analyze slows down the decision-making process and an organization may fail to react in time. The challenge is how to know which data is important, processing that data, and understanding what it means. Strategy-related decisions cannot, and should not, be made in a vacuum or based on gut instincts or intuition alone but should be developed based on the best available information at the time. Scenario planning offers a way of enabling complex decision-making by supporting the processing of information and filtering for insights that otherwise might go unnoticed. As the Canadian businessman, investor, and TV personality Robert Herjavec said, "Thinking too much leads to paralysis by analysis. It's important to think things through, but many use thinking as a means of avoiding action."

KEY SUB-COMPONENTS OF COMPLEX DECISION-MAKING

- Decision error mitigation
- Bounded rationality management
- Internal and external factors understanding
- Information stickiness
- Decision-making support

3. EDUCATIONAL (ORGANIZATIONAL) LEARNING

French physiologist Claude Bernard said, "It is what we think we know already that often prevents us from learning." Scenario planning offers a way to challenge mental models that have become ingrained in organizations and enable greater organizational learning. This has been found to give rise to all kinds of questions from a strategic point of view that would otherwise not be considered.

It's well known that learning organizations have several prime characteristics that enable success. These include a shared leadership vision, a strong organizational culture through relationships, and a sense of community. Learning organizations also have an organizational design that seems boundaryless with very few silos, allowing information to be shared freely among business units. Personal mastery is valued, and team learning occurs in all aspects of the business. Learning organizations also exhibit aspects of systems thinking, striving to understand the causal relationships among things and to change mental models, an undertaking that, as addressed in the previous chapter on complexity and uncertainty, aligns with the benefits of scenario planning.

Some companies, like Google, use their continuous learning culture and programs—like the "Googler to Googler" (peer-to-peer) training programs—as the key to overcoming anxiety related to technological disruption and uncertainty. Through this program, employees can sign up to deliver classes to colleagues on new skills they've mastered, a procedure that now accounts for approximately 55 percent of Google's classes. Disney took organizational learning in the context of customer experience to a new level three decades ago when it launched the Disney Institute, an organization geared to helping advise and train a variety of organizations worldwide based on the insight, experience, and leading practices of the Walt Disney Parks and Resorts.

Learning organizations also allow time for reflection, which is important when deciding on which strategy to follow. In an influential 2008 study, the late Harvard Business School scholar David Garvin talked about how supportive learning environments allow time for a pause in the action and encourage thoughtful review of the organization's processes. Garvin adds that leadership that reinforces learning typically occurs when leaders demonstrate a willingness to entertain alternative points of view and employees feel emboldened to offer new ideas.[13]

In addition, a learning organization constantly explores the process of continuous learning and has adaptive characteristics, according to another study by Thomas Chermack. In this paper, it is proposed that scenario planning helps create, enhance, and improve organizational learning. Although Chermack found mixed results with regard to the hard link between these two variables, they do outline a strong theoretical argument that, with further research, study, and exploration, has the potential to demonstrate something more plausible and conclusive.[14]

In contrast to the causal link between scenario planning and learning, Kees van der Heijden, associate fellow at Amsterdam's Said Business

School, focused on the balance between "strategizing" and "learning" and how both are required to navigate through complexity and uncertainty. Strategizing concerns prediction and control, making directional choices about the future, and solving problems. In contrast, learning concerns trying out new things, building capability, listening to others, natural selection (referring to continuous learning and adaptation over time), and knowing by participation (reflecting and testing what you've learned). Scenario planning supports both strategizing and learning but, more specifically, it enables leaders to consider alternative views by separating the strategic conversation of exploration from the actual decision-making process.

Van der Heijden describes a model of organizational learning as one that is multidimensional, involving a matrix that encompasses four categories of purpose: thinking and action as part of either an ongoing process or a one-off. Each combination involves different degrees of difficulty and likelihood of success, so van der Heijden advocates that organizations choose carefully the category they feel is most appropriate for them and adapt the process of scenario planning to support the chosen goal.

According to van der Heijden, anticipation occurs when scenario planning enables thinking as part of an ongoing process, and this has been found to enhance the level of the strategic conversation and a greater understanding of the external environment. Making sense of something involves developing specific questions for analysis, and an adaptive learning organization illustrates that there can be no true learning without action, so scenario planning cannot be purely thinking without doing.[15]

In times of major flux (complexity and uncertainty), van der Heijden has argued that scenario-based continual learning is the best strategy to identify and plan for external circumstances and prepare an organization to respond to them.

KEY SUB-COMPONENTS OF EDUCATIONAL LEARNING

- Continuous organizational learning
- Causal relationship understanding
- Anticipatory learning
- Internal capability development
- Collaboration and teaming

CASE STUDY
European Patent Office (The Future of IP Systems)

The European Patent Organisation is an intergovernmental organization established in 1973 to create a uniform patent system in Europe. The organization's operational agency is the European Patent Office (EPO). EPO, which provides a single unified procedure for patents for the 38 member states, is the largest international search authority, according to the UN-based Patent Cooperation Treaty. The office has over 7,000 employees, operates in three languages (English, French, and German), and is headquartered in Munich.

WHY AND HOW SCENARIO PLANNING WAS USED

EPO was part of the partnership between Shell, EDF, and the U.K. Health and Safety Board, which developed Risk2020 scenarios in the late 1990s. With some earlier history of success, EPO launched its own scenario project in 2004 to "look into the future of IP systems."

The process EPO conducted to develop scenarios was as follows:

1. A diverse group of 120 IP experts were interviewed.

2. Information was collected and four scenarios were devised that summarized the results clearly for stakeholders.

3. The final set of four scenarios were presented in 2007 to hundreds of IP experts and Chancellor Angela Merkel of Germany.

ORGANIZATIONAL BENEFITS AND RESULTS

Several benefits were experienced as a consequence of scenario planning at EPO. For example, after the second round of scenario planning, EPO was able to assist scientific stakeholders to be more receptive to **understanding the broader nature of uncertainty and complexity**. This was a key organizational learning outcome that occurred during the three-year planning process.

In addition, one of the scenarios outlined a fragmented global patent system that could lead to global trade conflicts. This scenario led EPO to increasingly integrate with international cooperative bodies, which included the Chinese. As a consequence, an institutional collaboration among the United States, Japan, China, South Korea, and EPO was established.

Finally, green technology received a brand-new patent classification scheme, including autonomous vehicles. Eighty of the salient interviews conducted in Phase 1 were published, and they communicated to staff and stakeholders that EPO was working in an unproductive environment that needed to change, while also demonstrating EPO's eagerness to **innovate**.[16]

4. NIMBLENESS

A nimble organization has a sustained ability to quickly and effectively respond to the needs of change from both the internal and external environments, while continually delivering results. Gaining and sustaining nimbleness is not easily achieved. Leaders in nimble organizations typically signal the organization's direction, enable action, and make quick and decisive decisions. The prioritization of work and allocation of resources also occurs very efficiently. Nimble organizations are able to sense and quickly seize on market opportunities. Teams have strong end-to-end accountabilities—people know what part they have to play in the system, boxes and lines are less important, and quick changes with flexible resource models are possible. Nimble organizations also tend to exhibit aspects of organizational learning and action-oriented decision-making as previously described.

It is accepted knowledge that larger organizations tend to lose elements of nimbleness and get bogged down with slow and overly bureaucratic processes. It's interesting to note that of the original Fortune 500 list published in 1955, only 12 percent of those companies still exist today. Large organizations like Digital Equipment Corp., Kodak, Blockbuster, and Ericsson were once considered the best in their field of play and thus likely to stay on top of the pack. They failed because they believed the external environment would remain the same. However, it is inevitable that there will be an economic disruption, or a competitor who gains in strength, or a new, formidable competitor that enters the market and takes over. When businesses fail, it is usually because they did not have the nimbleness to respond to change when it happened. Other organizations, like Haier Group of China, Mercedes-Benz, DuPont, Berkshire Hathaway, Coca-Cola, and newer firms like Microsoft, Google, Facebook, and Amazon, have retained the nimbleness of their start-up days and gone on to be very successful.

Scenario planning helps create a more agile and nimble organization capable of rapidly reacting and responding as drivers in the market change. Scenario planning builds enhanced strategic flexibility and prevents a rigid business plan that is not able to evolve and adapt as the environment changes.

Nimble organizations also typically have a sustained ability to both quickly and effectively respond to change while continually delivering business results: a two-track process. A good example of this is Apple, a firm that is highly dependent on computer chips for all its hardware devices, including the Mac and iPhone. Normally the company uses chips from Intel, but prior to Intel it used IBM, Motorola, and ARM Holdings. While this might suggest Apple was all over the place in its supplier choice, it was actually building nimbleness into its strategy. By not over-committing to one supplier, it ensured vendors stayed on top of the technology curve. Apple is looking into the future, seeing a range of potential scenarios, and trying to identify potential outcomes, keeping itself best positioned to win regardless of the outcome.[17]

KEY SUB-COMPONENTS OF NIMBLENESS

- Reacting and responding shorter term
- Adapting longer term
- Decision speed
- Strategic flexibility

5. ASSESSING UNCERTAINTY

Organizations exist within an external market, or sector, system that is influenced by political, economic, social, technological, environmental, and legal (PESTEL) macro forces. These have past, present, and future trends and characteristics that create uncertainty, mostly cannot be controlled, and need to be monitored. Organizations need to learn from the past and have a steady awareness of the present. Organizations also need to find ways, like scenario planning, to discover how to predict what might happen in the future at different levels of the system, while using the past and present as clues about the future.

In part, success for an organization rests on truly understanding the market or sector it operates within and the level of uncertainty that exists. According to BYU Marriott School of Business professor Jeff Dyer and a team of researchers, certain industries are plagued by more uncertainty than others, depending on the amount of technological uncertainty (industry R&D as a percentage of revenue) and demand uncertainty (index of industry revenue volatility and firm turnover). The report ranked medical equipment, computers, software, and pharmaceuticals as the most uncertain industries.[18]

Within the organization itself, strategies, processes, competencies, organizational structures, technologies, cultures, and competencies all create internal complexity that leaders have more control over and can manage in support of organizational products and services. The operating model of the organization serves to support the desired outcomes and the eventual performance and business results. Organizations are made up of people, from the lowest level of employees to managers and leaders, as described in the model below.

These three layers of the system (Market or Sector, Organization, and People) are illustrated in Figure 2 and demonstrate the interconnected nature of market, organization, and people and show sources of external uncertainty and internal complexity that need to be managed.

Chapter 2 described the characteristics of complexity and uncertainty in more detail and how organizations that fail to monitor these internal and external threats do so at their peril. The use of scenario planning enables organizations to monitor strategy execution by assessing and understanding environmental changes over time. For example, IBM has been generating its annual Global Technology Outlook report for 30 years. By updating its perspective on technology on a sustained basis, IBM's technological foresight has been enhanced.

FIGURE 2
Uncertainty and Complexity Within the System

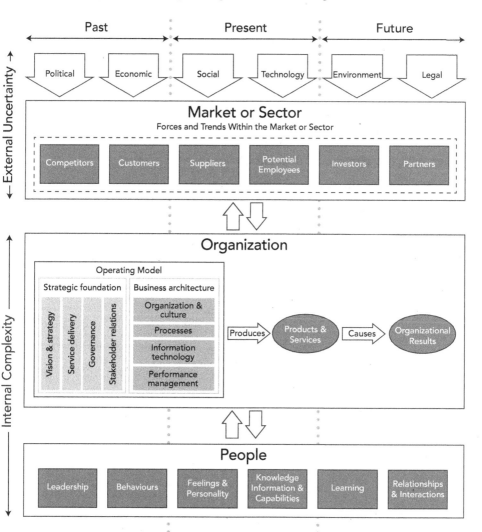

The literature on business complexity and environmental uncertainty, as well as its link to scenario planning, is extensive. Philip Walsh, School of Management, University of Surrey, defines it this way: when a firm finds itself in a changing environment, it must find a way to process all the information and create strategies to deal with all the changes. "Adaptive" organizations are those in which management is encouraged to identify changes in the environment through scenarios and make changes to their strategies and operating models. Scenario planning offers a mechanism to process large volumes of information and glean insights into the impact change will have on the business's strategy.[19]

In a world of increasing information, thinking becomes more important, and the ability to process the information is essential to success. "Systems thinking" is another relevant concept, described earlier, that enables the perception of reality from many different points instead of one. Systems thinking simplifies things by helping leaders see the patterns lying behind events. Good leaders who can use systems thinking have cognitive, emotional, and social intelligence.[20]

KEY SUB-COMPONENTS OF ASSESSING UNCERTAINTY

- Uncertainty and key market force monitoring
- Strategic anticipation
- Systems thinking
- Intelligent organization capability development

CASE STUDY
Ukupseni, Panama (Community Action Through Scenario Planning)

The community of Ukupseni is made up of 364 small islands, and at the time of the scenario planning process it had over 30,000 residents.

WHY AND HOW SCENARIO PLANNING WAS USED

In January 2007, community leaders in Ukupseni, Panama, were eager to explore the "future of the community in the face of social and ecological changes through the eyes of community members." In Ukupseni, the scenario planning process combined forecasting and back casting and followed the following format:

1. Outlined the objectives of the scenario planning research.

2. Collected information and major drivers of change by conducting structured interviews with participants across community demographics.

3. Crafted scenarios by using information derived from the interviews and preliminary research. During scenario development, the team used a Vision Scenario Matrix to help organize the drivers and uncertainty themes.

4. Combined forecasting and back-casting methods in order to provide as much community-wide collaboration as possible. Numerous workshops were run to collect the opinions of community members.

5. Made final revisions and released a report that included the scenario planning process and how the city would respond.

ORGANIZATIONAL BENEFITS AND RESULTS

From the scenarios, the city created different "visions" of what the scenarios might look like for certain community groups or demographics. From these visions, the city's team was able to properly understand how the same scenario could affect groups in different ways.

From the planning process, the city noted that people in the community felt "more comfortable and able to speak up and contribute to city planning." Overall, the city was more prepared for the future.[21]

6. RISK MANAGEMENT

With regard to risk management, scenario planning helps understand external risks, encourages leaders and teams to think about those risks or threats more deliberately, and enables a better understanding of the impacts those risks could have on the business. More specifically, "stretched" and unfavourable scenarios force organizations to consider those high-impact risks that otherwise might be overlooked. Ordinarily, as part of strategic planning processes, external risks are either never fully integrated into the process or ignored entirely in favour of internal risks. In 2007, the Canadian phone manufacturer Research in Motion (RIM) ignored the risk of Apple's iPhone as a competitor to RIM's BlackBerry, which had a superior operating system, strong market position, and 2 million customers. But, by 2013, RIM had been acquired by investors and broken up, while the iPhone took over the mobile phone market.[22]

Scenario planning also prompts questions about how resilient an organization is, measured by its ability to manage external risks. When trouble hits, what does it mean for the company? With accelerating and growing complexity and uncertainty, businesses are becoming less capable of identifying and mitigating the impact of risks.[23] However, there is a well-established link between scenario planning and managing risks, especially on large capital projects. According to Northeastern University's Todd Alessandri, scenario planning provides a structured way to manage risks, especially when the primary variables are not always quantifiable. Scenario planning helps identify longer-term risks that affect organizations.[24]

In 2015, Rolls-Royce, the British automobile and engine company, realized that it needed a way to prepare for an upcoming disaster after its share price dropped approximately 50 percent, the result of a perfect storm of factors. (These included a decline in demand for wide-body airliners, a drop in oil prices, the end of a commodities boom, and a slowing Chinese economy at a time when China was a significant customer.) Leaders set aside three days for scenario planning and an opportunity to discuss risks at length, research possible futures, create hypothetical scenarios, and then develop and refine a strategy.[25] Scenario planning has become an integral part of the Rolls-Royce strategy development process.

By considering all the potential risks that can affect business, organizations are better able to future-proof their strategies. It's important to not only identify the risks but also define mitigation strategies for each risk embedded within each scenario.

The future of newspapers in the digital age is an example of a sector experiencing tremendous challenges as a result of the development of online media. According to a 2016 article in *The Atlantic,* "Between 2000 and 2015, print newspaper advertising revenue fell from about $60-billion to about $20-billion, wiping out the gains of the previous 50 years." For more than a decade, traditional publishers and news outlets have been experimenting with various strategies to survive the digital revolution. According to reporter Julien Sueres in Medium.com, the ability to monetize news, which once had been a near-monopoly for newspaper owners, has become a source of incertitude and struggle. The implications are enormous: the loss of jobs for journalists, changes in audiences for advertising, and even the impact on quality and ethics for journalism in general.[26] Paul Schoemaker explains how scenario planning helps organizations systematically consider risks with a script-like characterization of possible futures and helps leaders become more aware of the potential risks they face so that management plans can be put into place.[27]

One further example of scenario planning helping mitigate risks is the New York Board of Trade. Its use of scenario planning led to a decision to build a second trading floor outside the World Trade Center, which kept the organization going after the events of 9/11.[28]

KEY SUB-COMPONENTS OF RISK MANAGEMENT
- Short-term risk identification
- Long-term risk identification
- Risk ranking
- Risk impact mitigation

7. INNOVATION

Innovation is the art of making hard things easy and creating value where it did not previously exist. Many organizations struggle to define innovation and lack a strategic approach to generating, capturing, and implementing innovative ideas. Innovation is a collaborative, structured process that involves different parts of the organization, as well as outside partners, to contribute, create and exploit new opportunities, and find new ways to solve complex problems. The sole action of generating ideas is not innovating. An idea becomes an innovation only when it has been implemented in a form that generates value.

A sound foundation for innovation should consist of six tightly integrated building blocks. Without a balance of these, efforts to build innovation will not stand. *Governance, culture,* and *people* sit at the core, but *strategy, process,* and the all-important *ideas* are equally critical.

As a tool that enhances an organization's ability to innovate, scenario planning is emerging as a proven benefit. It can help frame future aspirations, create a context for contingencies, and support innovative responses to strategic imperatives and current and future challenges. The question is whether this is true innovation or simply creative strategic responses. The RAND Corporation, an American global policy think tank, examined the future of transport scenarios to drive innovation in the United Kingdom. The roads in the United Kingdom are considered some of the most congested in the world, so the RAND Corporation applied scenario planning to help explore actions that would make transportation more efficient and effective. Its findings concluded that the United Kingdom should invest in robust technological interventions, develop policies to ensure that using new technologies results in measurable improvements, and support innovation in the form of autonomous vehicles and information and communications technology (ICT).

According to William Worthington, when considering the challenges of conducting business in an increasingly complex environment, the impact of "exogenous shocks" (external events that can destabilize strategies) has received growing attention.[29] Scenario planning is a tool to help firms translate their strengths into operational responses to react to, and recover from, exogenous shocks. Firms that adopt scenario planning techniques become more innovative in their responses to external challenges because they know it's a matter of survival.

Innovations can help support the types of products and services and the ways in which they are delivered, how an organization operates and functions, and how it deals with the external market. Innovation generates ideas and opportunities that provide continuous improvement. For example, the multinational investment firm Charles Schwab is known for being the first to define its niche market through continuous innovative practices attractive to individual customers. The organization is quick to perceive new market requirements and strives to be the "first mover" in innovative products to the investment community. Scenario planning can help generate these ideas, however big or small, through new mental models, new thinking, and new ways of approaching complexity and uncertainty.

Scenario planning also enables greater dynamic capability, with a focus more on identifying opportunities and less on mitigating risks. As an example, within the technology sector, innovation is a business imperative if a firm wants to survive for the long term. The impact on organizations of disruptive technologies in the market can be hard to identify and assess, and traditional mental models can lead to bias and blind spots among leaders, endangering strategic decision-making. Technology strategists are always looking for ways to stay ahead and remain well informed about emerging, rapidly changing technologies that could have both positive and negative impacts on businesses. Challenges include how to identify an opportunity for disruptive innovation at the early stages, how to gain the insight into likely development paths, and how to shape new technologies into opportunities for value creation and strategic advantage.[30]

Management scholar Stephen Drew explores how scenario planning directly enables strategic foresight within technology-driven organizations that need to predict potential future technology trends before they happen in order to more rapidly react and adapt. Scenario planning offers the ability to bring creativity into the planning process. Furthermore,

Drew outlines how scenario planning develops both discipline and imagination by building core capabilities in foresight, absorbing and managing knowledge, creative and strategic thinking, flexible decision-making and planning, and future-directed leadership.[31]

Another example of scenario planning enabling innovation is at the BMJ, a health care knowledge provider in the United Kingdom. Its leaders indicated that this management tool helped validate and stimulate innovation in its business. They explained how the tool combines creativity with an evidence-based approach as an art and a science using a comprehensive framework.[32]

British researchers David Sarpong and Mairi Maclean modify the claim that scenario planning leads directly to innovation, arguing that it helps organizations identify possibilities for innovation but not produce the innovation itself.[33]

KEY SUB-COMPONENTS OF INNOVATION

- Innovative strategic responses
- Creative thinking
- Technology-related strategic foresight
- Innovative initiative identification

8. OPTION ANALYSIS

As the psychologist and economist Daniel Kahneman once said, "The planning fallacy is that you make a plan, which is usually a best-case scenario. Then you assume that the outcome will follow your plan, even when you should know better." Scenario planning supports enhanced strategies by ensuring that more than one strategic option can be considered, leading to different paths that an organization can follow based on the external reality as opposed to just the best-case scenario. Scenario planning can be defined by leaders as something like a playbook, providing different chapters that represent different options for an organization to consider. As I have learned in my years of research and consulting, it offers both favourable and unfavourable options and forces leaders to consider the downside, worst-case scenario. It provides a tool to explore alternative futures in a world where volatility is high, a tool that stretches perspectives and tests the resilience of a company against those alternative futures.

Moving from strategy to execution, scenario planning encourages teams to articulate the different actions that could be taken under different conditions, making sure the assets and portfolio structure, but also the wider corporate structure, is challenged to ensure it's diversified and organized in the right way to weather the possible futures. Scenario planning removes bias from the strategy process, since many organizations suffer from "CEO ego" (the perception that these leaders have all the answers), which in many cases is not correct.

Organizations make decisions all the time and don't always consider, or are aware of, the broader options available to them, and even when they do understand the potential options, those options are not always properly evaluated in the process. Success is about understanding what the strategic options are and having enough information at that time to make an informed decision that maximizes results.

By considering multiple options, organizations build the capability to identify and manage changes in the external environment and quickly commit resources to a new course of action in response. In a highly uncertain and complex environment, managers need to have this option. Researchers Katsuhiko Shimizu, from Keio University in Tokyo, and Michael Hitt, from Texas A&M University, describe several barriers to strategic flexibility, including organizational insensibility to negative feedback, a condition where managers ignore early signs of strategic mistakes, and a self-serving interpretation of negative feedback leading to uncertainty and resistance causing lack of action.[34]

Two scholars, David Aaker at the University of California, Berkeley's business school and Briance Mascarenhas, from New York University's School of Business, describe option analysis, or strategic flexibility, as the ability of an organization to adapt to substantial, uncertain, and fast-occurring changes that have meaningful impact on performance. Their research goes beyond explaining what it is and specifically defines three approaches to maintaining strategic flexibility, including diversification strengths, investment in underused resources, and reduced commitment to resources to specialized uses. Each firm should decide which option makes the most sense given its individual context and make decisions on investments related to R&D, finance, operations, marketing, and sales. By considering a wider range of options, leaders are encouraged to expand their thinking.[35]

Again, according to Aaker and Mascarenhas, organizations initially build scenarios of the future by identifying the major change drivers and the range of possible futures and determine which are the most plausible. They then formulate optimal strategies for each scenario and determine the best strategic options, define the core elements of the strategy that don't change irrespective of the scenario, and decide on those elements within the strategy that change or are optional for each scenario. Once the strategy is made operational, leaders start to manage the portfolio of options, monitor the environment, determine which strategic option is appropriate, and stick with the core elements of the strategy.

KEY SUB-COMPONENTS OF OPTION ANALYSIS
- Strategic options
- Diversification exploration
- Investment in underused resources
- Reduced commitment to resources to specialized uses

SCENARIO PLANNING BENEFIT MODEL

Considering the existing research and examples outlined in the previous section and reasons businesses perform scenario planning, I have identified eight potential benefits. These benefits are further illustrated in a new benefit model, outlined below, including a set of sub-components that go with each benefit.

FIGURE 3
Specific Scenario Planning Benefit Model

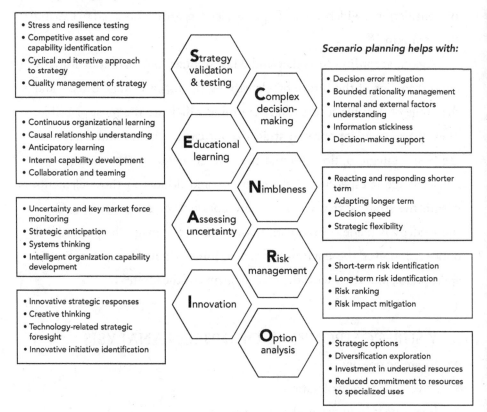

Scenario planning helps with:

- Stress and resilience testing
- Competitive asset and core capability identification
- Cyclical and iterative approach to strategy
- Quality management of strategy

- Continuous organizational learning
- Causal relationship understanding
- Anticipatory learning
- Internal capability development
- Collaboration and teaming

- Uncertainty and key market force monitoring
- Strategic anticipation
- Systems thinking
- Intelligent organization capability development

- Innovative strategic responses
- Creative thinking
- Technology-related strategic foresight
- Innovative initiative identification

Strategy validation & testing

Educational learning

Assessing uncertainty

Innovation

Complex decision-making

Nimbleness

Risk management

Option analysis

Scenario planning helps with:

- Decision error mitigation
- Bounded rationality management
- Internal and external factors understanding
- Information stickiness
- Decision-making support

- Reacting and responding shorter term
- Adapting longer term
- Decision speed
- Strategic flexibility

- Short-term risk identification
- Long-term risk identification
- Risk ranking
- Risk impact mitigation

- Strategic options
- Diversification exploration
- Investment in underused resources
- Reduced commitment to resources to specialized uses

These eight benefit components can be broadly grouped into three categories: (a) **input benefits,** which essentially help understand the external environment through assessing the uncertainty and risk management involved with extraordinary events, like COVID-19; (b) **process benefits,** which outline the consequences of a greater understanding of external uncertainties and risks, and include educational learning, option analysis and strategy validation, and testing; and (c) **output benefits,** which result from the educational learning, option analysis, and strategy validation process and which include complex decision-making, nimbleness (strategic flexibility), and innovation.

In summary, the specific benefits that will occur within an organization depend on the context of the organization and also on what it is trying to achieve. For example, highly innovative companies in the technology space may decide to use scenario planning as a way of driving innovation, whereas, say, a mining company might care more about considering future risks that the organization is exposed to, such as commodity prices.

Another consideration is the type of strategic intervention the organization is trying to make. For example, most organizations use elements of scenario planning to help understand what possible futures could look like so that they can take strategic action to survive or even thrive in that environment. However, what progressive organizations look to achieve through scenario planning is to understand the future so that it can be influenced and manipulated to their advantage through new system relationships that perhaps did not previously exist.

There is no right or wrong answer, but what's important is taking a deliberate process to using scenario planning and understanding what it is you want it to help you with, based on the context of your business and the challenges it faces.

■ ■ ■

SUMMARY KEY POINTS

- Scenario planning supports several benefits in organizations.
- Scenario planning helps stress-test the viability of current strategies, ensure resilience, and future-proofs and helps to review strategy on an iterative basis.
- Scenarios can be used for various levels of complex decision-making, including making a decision on a specific strategic issue, setting a high-level strategic agenda, assessing risks and opportunities, considering multiple market drivers, and understanding the worst-case scenario while making decisions.
- Scenario planning enhances educational learning (organizational learning) through the understanding of the causal relationships between variables in the system, anticipatory learning, continuous learning, collaboration, and teaming.
- Scenario planning helps create more agile and nimble organizations that are capable of reacting and responding as drivers in the market change, can build enhanced strategic flexibility, and prevents a rigid business plan that is not able to evolve and adapt with changes and uncertainties in the market conditions.
- Scenario planning enables businesses to monitor strategy execution by assessing environmental changes and uncertainties over time and understanding what they mean and better anticipating what might happen.
- Scenario planning produces a more complete and rigorous plan by considering all the adverse risks that can affect the business, identifying each risk and defining risk mitigation strategies in advance.

- Different scenarios help to frame future aspirations, create a context for contingencies, develop innovative responses to strategic imperatives and current and future challenges, and consider emerging technologies that might not be fully developed but are coming.
- Scenario planning supports enhanced strategies by helping ensure more than one strategic option is considered and mapping different paths an organization can follow based on the external reality.
- The benefits of scenario planning are integrated and related and not mutually exclusive.
- The benefits will vary depending on the organization's situation and context.

CHAPTER 6

CRITICAL ROLES TO DRIVE SUCCESS

"If you don't contradict yourself on a regular basis, then you're not thinking."

—MALCOLM GLADWELL, AUTHOR

To combat increasing uncertainties and risks, businesses must adopt a strategic mindset to approach competition, the market, and the rest of their business realities and look beyond the present to predict what changes, risks, and disruptions might lie in the future.

The chief executive officer (CEO) and chief strategy officer (CSO) (or VP Strategy in some organizations) play an important role in driving strategy and leveraging the benefits of scenario planning with the support of the scenario planning team. All CEOs and most CSOs are involved in the upfront part of the development process of strategy, leaving execution to specific business units and functional leaders to ensure it is successfully implemented and that it cascades down to front-line employees.

This chapter is concerned less with the *how*, as explained in Chapters 3 and 4, and more with the *who*, specifically the roles of the CEO and CSO in scenario planning as part of a wider strategy development process. Furthermore, we look at a breakdown of what attributes and crucial success factors contribute to the making of an excellent CEO and CSO. This chapter also tackles more briefly the role of scenario planners in coordinating the process, bringing it to life, and acting as its engines of execution.

THE ROLE OF THE CEO

According to outplacement firm Challenger, Gray, & Christmas, the year 2019 had the highest number of CEO departures on record since monitoring began in 2002: more than 1,600. Among the more high-profile departures was Boeing CEO Dennis Muilenburg, who was fired in December 2019 as a consequence of the 737 Max 8 crisis.[1] In today's business context, organizations cannot settle for mediocre performance; they must periodically undergo transformations to maintain results and shareholder returns through a constantly enhanced strategy. The questions that relate to scenario planning are these: What exactly should CEOs be doing? How should they be involved? How do they ensure the right behaviours among those at the top table? Whom should they involve?

The role of CEOs is unique in that they stand at the top of the organization, and everyone below them takes direction from this one individual. Only the CEO can ensure that the right people spend the right amount of time undertaking the necessary actions within. The CEO plays a critical role overseeing the process of scenario planning and that of the broader strategy development. Ultimately the CEO owns the strategy, sets the tone from the top, and is responsible for the vision and mission of the company.

The CEO must buy into the importance of scenario planning, otherwise it will not be successful. Leaders will not support it, and challenges will occur when trying to communicate the results to front-line workers.

The CEO also needs to demonstrate personal involvement in the process, dedicating the right specialist resources to the task and supporting changes in thinking among senior leaders regarding decision-making, strategy validation, and risk management.

All CEOs are different, bringing to their role special and unique experiences, personalities, and preferences. That is what, in part, makes them so interesting, but there are a set of important, common roles or modes that CEOs have to combine when promoting scenario planning:

- **The Innovator:** CEOs, more than anyone else in the organization, play an important role in driving change and helping others consider how external uncertainties, risks, and threats identified through scenario planning could be a source of opportunity in the future. CEOs also drive culture, can form new partnerships, and bring change agents into the organization to encourage innovation, forcing others to get outside their comfort zones and interact with disruptors.
  - In practice: Some CEOs put their executive leadership teams through innovation workshops to expand thinking. Others lead tours of Silicon Valley and arrange meetings with venture capitalists to identify emerging technologies or potential disruptors. In addition, some run structured relationships with university incubators and innovation labs.

- **The Communicator:** CEOs need to communicate consistently throughout the organization in a way that recognizes the importance of scenario planning and factors in external risk, uncertainty, and internal complexity as part of the strategy development process. The CEO should also communicate the importance of organizational learning, strategic flexibility and nimbleness, and other beneficial aspects of the process.

- In practice: Communicators should not only celebrate successes but also discuss why an idea or effort didn't work and explore the lessons learned from that experience. Messages need to be frequently repeated to employees to ensure they sink in. At Zappos, former CEO Tony Hsieh treated employees as his most important audience with transparent and open communications in a way that broke down silos, allowing employees to raise issues.[2] Zappos, which was acquired by Amazon in 2009 in a deal valued at $1.2 billion, is considered exceptional when it comes to customer service and being one of the best places to work.

- **The Personable:** CEOs who take time to get to know people, at the leadership table and further down in the organization, tend to have greater success when trying to drive new initiatives and management tools like scenario planning. The CEO needs to dumb it down to simple, easily understood concepts and explain why it's important to consider external risks, uncertainties, and threats. Wherever possible, it's advantageous to explain the message through stories. The power of a story can be very effective in unblocking employee energy. To make it even more memorable, personalizing the story forces CEOs to consider and share with others the desired message using simple, easily understood language that has real meaning to the individual.

  Within the scenario planning process, CEOs play an important role in discussing with the top team what the scenarios mean to the organization, encouraging debate about the different futures, reinforcing a particular opinion, and prompting leaders to articulate their thoughts, concerns, and actions (how they would react in different situations).

  - In practice: Some leaders include examples from their own life experiences to underscore their determination and focus on doing something new—and to demonstrate that obstacles can be overcome and success will prevail. For example, Bob Chapman, the CEO of Barry-Wehmiller, a global supplier of manufacturing technology and services, explains in his book *Everybody Matters—The Extraordinary Power of Caring for Your People Like Family* how since the early 2000s he has focused on bringing out the best in his employees through trust, continuous improvement, freedom, communication, and respect.[3]

- **The Role Model:** The CEO is expected to act as a role model for the desired behaviours, especially as part of the strategy development and scenario planning process. This includes exhibiting the right attitudes and behaviours when discussing complex decisions, external risks and uncertainties, and internal complexity. The CEO should be the one most amenable to enhanced mental models and broader thinking. As the organization's chief role model, others will be looking to the CEO for cues.

  - In practice: In discussions with top leaders, the CEO needs to create an environment of healthy conflict and challenge, but also support. The team members need to believe in the process and not be afraid of the doomsday scenario.

- **The Doer:** There are times when CEOs need to roll up their sleeves and show the way forward, which is not to be confused with micromanaging. Doing this at points in the process has tremendous symbolic value; others will observe and take their cues from it. It shows that CEOs are personally invested in the process, believe in its importance, and are encouraging others to get on board. At times, doing this can accelerate the process, ensure decisions get quickly made, and, when debate is endlessly ongoing, help bring things to a conclusion.

- In practice: When translating the results of scenario planning dialogues into strategic initiatives, there may be times when an individual, or members of a business unit, may be unclear about the initiative. These moments offer opportunities for leaders to step in and take the time to explain.

CEO CRITICAL SUCCESS FACTORS

In addition to the inherent characteristics that make a CEO successful in supporting the organization-wide scenario planning process, the individual's specific skills, experiences, and relationships are also instrumental in driving success. Some of these include the following:

1. **Creating a sense of urgency.** Author and renowned speaker Bob Proctor said, "Everyone should have a sense of urgency—it is getting a lot done in a short period of time in a calm confident manner." It's important to never rest on your past successes, but always challenge yourself and your organization to do more and do better, particularly in an environment of accelerating uncertainty and complexity. A continued sense of urgency to understand, explore, and exploit the external and internal environment is what makes CEOs successful, especially when considering the application of scenario planning within the organization. CEOs need to continually find ways to insert urgency and disruptive thinking within an organization; encourage leaders to expand current mental models; consider external risks, threats, and uncertainties; and uncover internal complexities that hinder growth. The disruption that you least expect could be just around the corner so you need to be prepared and have the appropriate shock absorbers in place. John Kotter, an author and

professor at the Harvard Business School, wrote in his 2008 book *A Sense of Urgency* that *"true urgency* is a gut-level determination to *move and win, now.* Its practitioners ... *come to work each day determined* to *achieve something important,* and *they shed irrelevant activities* to *move faster* and *smarter."* He also wrote: "Those with a sense of urgency are the opposite of complacent.... Instead, they move boldly toward the future—sharply on the lookout for the hazards and the opportunities that change brings."[4]

2. **Learning from failure.** Learning from failed past strategic attempts is critical to success. CEOs play a role in changing perspectives on what failure means and turning it into a positive experience, where failures occur quickly and are seen as valuable learning events. When conducting scenario planning exercises, the organizational learning process is an important aspect of planning for multiple futures, and a full understanding of past decisions is viewed as valuable input even in cases where they did not work. Organizational learning also encourages more innovative ideas and agile product and service development, as well as facilitates diverse thinking that can be further explored as an outcome of the scenario planning process.

3. **Ensuring a diversity of talent to expand thinking.** Many organizational leadership teams suffer from "group think" with a one-dimensional view of external risks, uncertainties, and threats because of a lack of diverse thinking at the top table. As part of a scenario planning process, CEOs play an important role in ensuring expanded thinking occurs, especially when complex strategic decisions need to be made; they have the power and authority to mix things up by asking basic questions like, "Could this happen? If it did happen, what would we do?" Changing the organization's talent mix, both

at the leadership level and farther down the ladder provides another important lever for ensuring the future strategy is properly stress-tested and validated, and also future-proofed for all possible realities. Criteria such as an ability to innovate, openness to change, disruptive thinking, diversity of ideas, and entrepreneurialism are all important traits when having the dialogue on scenarios. CEOs also seek to recruit talent who have experienced disruption in other sectors and come without entrenched biases and assumptions.

4. **Measuring and incentivizing.** As the saying goes, "You are what you measure," and if CEOs want the top team to embrace scenario planning and all the related benefits and consequences of this tool, they have to measure the individual performances of those involved against agreed-upon expectations. What is expected: active and engaged participation in workshops; ongoing execution and implementation of results; and cascading of scenarios to business units and functions like HR, IT, and Finance. Also, incorporating expanded mental models, as well as broader external and internal thinking, needs to become part of the norm for all leaders. Defining the behaviours that lead to rewards and recognition aligns the organization to the desired culture.

5. **Making scenario planning meaningful.** Performing the required research on trends, risks, and uncertainties, and developing scenarios and properly stress-testing and validating strategies requires tremendous effort. Leaders must fundamentally rethink and reshape the future of the business by considering possible and plausible futures while continuing to run the business day to day. Where does this energy come from? Powerful scenarios told through a story help leaders believe in the effort by answering their big questions about what the possible futures could look like, what big risks

and uncertainties could fundamentally disrupt the business, and what strategic actions the organization can take to adapt and react should a particular scenario play out. A scenario's impact on an organization will depend on not just having compelling depictions of the future but also the CEO's willingness and ability to make things personal and to engage others in a meaningful way through the process. According to a report by Forbes, many organizations re-examine their long-term strategies on an annual basis. While a CEO may delegate process management to someone like the head of strategic planning or CFO, a CEO must be intimately involved in key decisions. If vision and values are the CEO's number-one job, strategy is a close second.[5]

6. **Highlighting success stories.** As the development and implementation of scenario planning progresses within an organization, it's important to highlight successes as they occur. This is a powerful way to reinforce why you are doing something a particular way. Sharing these success stories helps reinforce the meaning of scenario planning and gives people confidence that it should be used as it cascades down through an organization. It also builds momentum by showcasing results in real time.

7. **Building a strong and committed executive team.** How the members of the executive leadership team within an organization behave and work together through any strategic conversations and activities is critical to success. Scenario planning–based discussions can be tough, stretching leaders to think about very unfavourable situations that could create tremendous strain on the company. The ability to have frank and open dialogues about these challenges and what they mean, leaving power and politics at the door, is an

essential part of the process. But the executive team also needs to think as one, limit any lone-wolf syndrome, and, while possibly disagreeing in the room, return to the organization aligned on a decision and with an unambiguous message to employees. The process of performing scenario planning can be a valuable team-building exercise.

8. **Investing the time in the process.** Strategy-related dialogues and the exploration of scenarios that impact an organization cannot be rushed and require many group workshops. As part of the planning process, it's important that the leaders agree on how much time they will spend together and the type of outcomes expected, and ensure everyone commits to be part of the process. Even when facilitated by experts, the leaders need to be engaged and actively participating in the process. With the right team in place ready to discuss the scenarios, it still takes time for a group of high-performing, intelligent, ambitious, and independent people to align themselves behind a set of scenarios and related strategies. According to a report by McKinsey, collective motivation, enthusiasm, and intense commitment are crucial ingredients of a successful transformation of any kind, and there is no substitute for a CEO directing his or her personal energy toward ensuring that the company's efforts have an impact.[6]

    To ensure a leadership team has effective dialogues about the scenarios, there needs to be a well-planned and structured agenda, with the right input and research going into the process to ensure the sessions are well executed and based on good information. It's also important to think about how the time is managed, allowing for personal reflection, discussion in small groups, and discussions as a wider leadership team. Face-to-face meetings are preferred to maximize the level of commitment and engagement and to be able to quickly recalibrate if the discussion begins going down rabbit holes.

9. **Relentlessly pursuing results.** The whole point of doing scenario planning in an organization is to have an impact on the company's results and the success of the strategy under different situations. CEOs need to focus on two goals: making the company better and achieving enhanced business results. CEOs have both the opportunity and the power to put all their energy, commitment, and enthusiasm behind the process, inspiring other leaders and employees to follow their lead. CEOs have to hold others accountable for results, as well as for the process itself (the resulting strategies and initiatives) and the cascading down of the expected results throughout the organization at the business-unit, functional, and project level. CEOs also help ensure that decision-making, which can be complex, is grounded in the information, both internal and external, that is relevant to the organization. Finally, CEOs may need to make judgment calls to ensure that the process moves from theoretical to practical with a strong grounding in numbers attached to each scenario.

CASE STUDY
The BMJ (Understanding the Changing Dynamics of Global Research)

The BMJ, formally the British Medical Journal, is a health care knowledge provider that publishes medical journals, provides professional development resources, and delivers evidence-based decision-support tools. The BMJ is headquartered in the United

Kingdom but has offices in other parts of the world. The BMJ is owned by the British Medical Association (BMA).

WHY AND HOW SCENARIO PLANNING WAS USED

The world is currently in the era of "hyper competition" in publishing and knowledge services, with added complexity because of technological disruption and new players entering the market. This environment propelled the BMJ to engage its entire organization to think on the same level about changing dynamics in the industry. The BMJ set out to develop scenarios to "understand how global research might evolve over the next 20 years and in what ways this may disrupt their business." In 2016 the BMJ began its scenario planning process, which comprised several phases:

1. Developed a specific team to meet every fortnight, which would spearhead the scenario planning project throughout the organization.

2. Gained senior leadership support, including the board of directors, and sought advice from other organizations that had scenario planned in the past, such as the Royal Chemistry Society.

3. Conducted 50 internal and external interviews, and then highlighted three global trends and six global research themes.

4. Presented three workshops with different themes in order to devise four scenarios; 20 internal executive leaders and managers engaged in these workshops.

ORGANIZATIONAL BENEFITS AND RESULTS

The BMJ Open Science, an innovative new journal, was directly informed by its scenario planning process, and new research needs were considered and identified.

The BMJ took on an investment proposal strategy in which its investment must "deliver profits for the next three years and align with future business models." The latter clause was supported by the scenario planning process, which assisted decision-makers in their complex investment decisions.

Both incoming and outgoing CEOs participated in the process. Their support played a critical role in ensuring the success of the scenario planning effort, including a slot in the monthly CEO video. The BMJ also engaged the members of its board of directors, who provided vital steering for the next steps and regularly recommended exploring new topics. In addition, the company's acquisition strategy was shaped by an organization-wide better understanding of how the company fits into the external operating environment.

A final benefit was the internal communication and organizational learning process, which was sparked by the scenario planning and led to cross-company ideation meetings in order to promote innovation.

The BMJ prepared a "pre-read," which was a comprehensive 25-page report that identified the critical global research themes that may impact the future. The "pre-read" supplemented the participants' knowledge of the future and helped spark conversation throughout the process.[7,8]

THE ROLE OF THE CSO

Based on experience in a variety of strategy functions, coupled with survey results and interviews with various executives, I found a number of roles or modes that make for a successful and high-performing chief strategy officer (CSO) in the context of enabling and supporting scenario planning within an organization.[9] Although finding someone who ticks all these boxes is unlikely, the following should be used as considerations when looking for a CSO, taking into account the requirements of the scenario planning process.

- **The Anticipator:** Understanding and anticipating marketplace trends, risks, and uncertainties is an important quality, as is forward-thinking and future-thinking. Such a person often asks "What's next" when thinking of advances. He or she always has a finger on the pulse of the multi-faceted external and internal business environments and is ready to react and adapt. According to a report by Deloitte in the United States, one of the six indispensable roles of a CSO is as the "Sentinel," an individual who has the ability to monitor market shifts and swiftly act on them. Senior leaders expect CSOs to have their eyes and ears open and apprise them of potentially threatening competitive changes.[10]
  - In practice: Look for someone well-read who stays on top of current business, economic, industry, technological, legal, social, and political trends; someone who looks for signals on how the future might play out.

- **The Disruptor:** Constantly challenging the status quo of an organization's strategic position, playing devil's advocate, and challenging the organization to think broadly and stay agile and open to change as well as new ideas are hallmarks of the Disruptor. They observe external changes affecting the organization and explore how they can be powerful catalysts for internal evolution and innovation with regard to new strategies.
  - In practice: The Distruptor creates a safe environment where thoughts can be freely shared by participants, but also asks

leadership the tough questions as part of the scenario planning process—What if, why not? What's stopping you? Have you thought of this? Could this happen? What would be the impact? He or she fearlessly challenges the status quo to ensure the organization covers all strategic bases, creating the right amount of tension and friction to be able to execute challenging work. According to a report in the *Harvard Business Review,* a great CSO is one who goes beyond leading the traditional annual strategic planning process, which typically struggles to absorb the shocks and disruptions of today's uncertain and complex markets. This is an individual who can transform an ongoing process with continual discussions about the strategy among different groups of people.[11]

- **The Learner:** Learners have a natural curiosity that will bring in new ideas and insights through scenario planning to help further develop the organization. They are comfortable with ambiguity, adapting and thriving in unfamiliar environments to gain understanding and insight on how to successfully navigate uncharted territory and potential future realities. They embrace organizational learning and use the scenario planning process to facilitate this learning as part of the approach.
  - In practice: The Learner joins industry associations and industry groups to learn about trends, risks, uncertainties, and leading practices in other sectors. The most relevant ideas are brought back and shared with leadership through the wider strategic planning and specific scenario planning process.

- **The Adapter:** The ability to wear multiple hats and adapt to playing different roles simultaneously defines Adapters. They can quickly switch between tasks, adjust to changes in the business environment, and stay flexible as external and internal conditions change. They nimbly change course and focus to enable the company to do the same.

- In practice: One minute the Adapter is preparing for an off-site executive leadership team's scenario planning session and the next is assessing strategic acquisitions. Adapters stay versatile and adaptable to the organization's many strategic needs and encourage flexibility as part of scenario thinking.

- **The Storyteller:** Storytellers are capable of articulating the importance of the strategy across layers in the organization, connecting the dots to help everyone understand the "why" in strategic decisions. They defend decisions to investors and board members using a compelling narrative to gain support and build alignment. Scenarios are used to tell different stories about potential futures, both favourable and unfavourable, to ensure ultimate preparedness. The more compelling the story, the more enthusiasm and energy the Storyteller can generate among stakeholders. The common elements of a great story are simplicity, familiarity, reliability, and drama. Jennifer Aaker, a professor at the Stanford Graduate School of Business, said, "Our brains are wired to understand and retain stories. Story is a journey that moves the listener, and when the listener goes on that journey they feel different and the result is persuasion and sometimes action."[12]

  - In practice: Storytellers take all the facts and details used in formulating the scenarios and turn them into a powerful story that engages and compels leaders, employees, and investors to buy in.

- **The Translator:** Adapting to different tasks and translating insights from research performed by scenario planners to the executive team are characteristics of Translators. They are constantly scanning and learning about external changes and challenges and then interpreting these learnings to make them understandable and relevant.

● In practice: Translators act as the link between the high-level scenario plan and the simple processes and tools that empower business units and functions to execute the scenario plan.

● **The Navigator:** Like the person who directs the course of a ship, the Navigator proactively manages the organization's strategic direction, always keeping the team headed for its destination while navigating the rough waters of internal resistance and external change. Navigators know who and when to ask for assistance, specifically in areas that may be outside the company's expertise and particularly related to external threats. They instinctively know when to change direction and how to find an alternative route to success based on scenario analysis.

● In practice: Navigators set the long-term strategic objectives and help the leadership team understand short- and medium-term objectives. They develop a clear, realistic, prioritized, and sequenced road map that supports execution of the strategy.

● **The Integrator:** Integrators build consensus with executive leadership and the broader organization about the right direction for the company while leveraging the scenario planning process. Individual silos within an organization, such as business units and other functions, each have their own objectives and metrics that they need to achieve. The Integrator can, and should, play a role in helping ensure those goals are met and are also aligned with the organization's common goal. Another role is bringing cross-functional teams together to support company-wide issues.

- In practice: The role integrates many moving parts between different leaders—bringing together strategy, strategic planning, scenario planning and enterprise risk management (chief risk officer), with M&A (corporate development officer), the budget and forecast (chief financial officer), and with workforce strategy (human resources officer).

- **The Influencer:** Influencers scan the environment for new information and challenge the organization to stretch its thinking and mental models beyond what feels safe and comfortable. They stand as the strategy's ultimate champion and persuade others to take threats, risks, market trends, uncertainties, and opportunities seriously.
  - In practice: They build credibility by spending large amounts of time with business-unit and functional leaders engaging, listening, and collaborating on strategy development and execution. They avoid the black-box syndrome of working in isolation on strategy for a "big reveal."

CSO CRITICAL SUCCESS FACTORS

In addition to the inherent characteristics that make a successful CSO, the individual's specific skills, experiences, and relationships are also instrumental in driving success. These include the following:

1. **Rapport with CEO.** The CSO should feel comfortable enough to challenge the CEO's thinking, mental models, and decision-making approach, but they should otherwise be in lockstep with each other on strategy development and execution. The CEO is the ultimate owner of the strategy that gets tested through the scenario planning

process and is responsible for its execution. If the CEO and CSO aren't aligned, there's no way for the strategy to be approved by the board and rolled out successfully across the organization. If that happens, the CSO risks being sidelined by the CEO.

2. **Appropriate role scope.** A CSO's duties will depend on the size of the organization and the complexity of the industry. The breadth of duties from a strategy and scenario planning perspective should be fine-tuned to these unique circumstances. All other executive team members should clearly understand what is in and out of scope for the CSO. CSOs in smaller organizations need to undertake a broader set of tasks, while those in larger organizations need to be deliberate and specific in the tasks they take on and avoid undertaking so much that they'll be unable to do their best. In the context of scenario planning, an appropriate breadth of responsibilities allows a CSO to be most effective by doing a few things very well instead of doing many things poorly. This workload needs to be defined and agreed upon with the executive team from the start. It's also important that other executives don't feel that their responsibilities are being encroached on and there is strong alignment.

3. **Deliberate role definition.** Defining the role and clearly stating from the beginning what is required of the CSO is crucial to success. Without proper discussion and deliberation in outlining the CSO's role, there will likely be a mismatch between the CSO and the executive team. For example, defining the role of the CSO as it relates to the facilitation of scenario-related workshops and cascading scenarios into specific business units, functions, and capital projects should be completed.

4. **Strong financial acumen.** The CSO must have the financial acumen to stay grounded and understand the feasibility of the strategy, and to interpret data and make decisions informed by the numbers. A strong relationship with the CFO is integral to successful strategy development. The CSO has to build realistic strategies that can be executed to meet stakeholder expectations, including shareholders. A CSO who is aware and understands the financial realities can build these realities into strategic decisions. Although scenarios at the corporate level tend to be qualitative in nature, they increasingly become quantitative as they get translated down to the business-unit or functional level.

5. **Tactical understanding.** Although scenario planning has an inherent focus on the future, a CSO needs to have a tactical understanding of what needs to be done now, in the present, to deliver value. The CSO must be able to play a role in the company's short-, medium-, and long-term direction. Understanding and reacting to present circumstances is a large part of long-term strategic thinking. It allows for short-term, tactical decisions and reactions to immediate changes in the business environment that are aligned with a company's long-term vision developed through future-focused scenarios. Forward-looking plans will be realized only when momentum has built up through tactical decisions, and the CSO needs to understand the short-term steps needed to achieve the longer-term vision.

6. **Fluent in technology advances.** CSOs must be up to date on digital advances that will affect their organizations and understand the importance of digital to the organization's productivity, connectivity, and competitiveness. A close working relationship with the chief

information officer/chief data officer/chief digital officer is helpful here. Today, technology has the power to radically disrupt the way an organization operates, creating a huge amount of risk and uncertainty, so the digital strategy is crucial to the broader company strategy. Disruption is happening regardless of whether a company moves forward or sticks its head in the sand. As indicated in a *Harvard Business Review* report, more than half of CSOs surveyed said they are spending more and more time looking at issues within the IT and digital domains, which are not traditional strengths of CSOs.[13]

7. **Strong people engagement skills.** Given the high degree of stakeholder engagement required in the scenario planning process, the ability to engage a variety of stakeholders through strong people skills is critical to success. Scenario planning and strategy development processes require a high degree of group workshop–style exercises, where the ability to listen, connect, interpret, and align different viewpoints ensures a more successful process.

The staggering pace of change in today's business landscape causes massive disruption for many industries, increasing the strategic complexity for companies as they try to stay relevant. Consumer demands have increased, with calls for improved personalization, social advocacy, and environmental responsibility. Global shifts have meant bigger players are competing on an international stage, drawing efficiencies through M&A activities around the world.

Alongside all this change, rapid advances in digital technology have upended some industries entirely, causing business models to change and industries to converge. Digital change will only continue to accelerate, with greater change still to come with advancements in artificial intelligence. Operating in this increasingly complex and changing environment has made an organization's strategy more important than ever.

To meet this increased demand for an adaptable and coherent strategy, organizations must have a senior leader who is focused on strategic direction and potential futures that could play out: the CSO. This role is crucial for companies today, and business leaders must be selective in whom they choose for the position. The CSO will play a central role in how the company understands the changing business landscape, assess what's important to know internally and externally, and filter the external noise. When this is done, the CSO can steer the company toward the future in both the short and long term.

DIFFERENT CSO ROLES

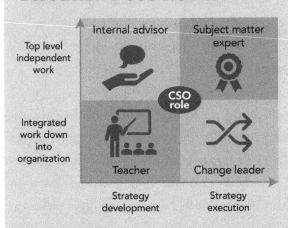

Strong role definition is critical to the CSO's success, with a "right-sized" role for the organization and industry, and a defined working relationship with the rest of the executive team. The decision of whether the CSO will play a more independent or integrated role in the business, and whether it will be more in strategy formulation or implementation, are considerations that will require some thought by the executive team. What makes the most sense in the organization's unique context? Once the CSO role is defined, it's more likely the CSO will succeed.

While the executive team faces increased pressure from investors, consumers, and governments, it's up to the CSO to think about the organization's long-term focus and rally the rest of the company around it, using management tools like scenario planning. With such a broad task, the CSO must wear multiple hats, not only being plugged into the state of the world but also being able to think innovatively and translate relevant information, insights, and ideas to the rest of the executive team and from there down through the organization. A study by the consulting group BCG found that strategic planning, growth, and business model innovation are the fundamental responsibilities of almost every CSO. Through the planning process, effective CSOs provide top-down guidance to the business units and align those units' plans with those of the corporate centre.[14]

Being the person accountable for strategy in an organization, the CSO must take a holistic, end-to-end approach. A CSO with an intimate understanding of the dimensions of the strategic framework will enable prioritization of the areas that matter most for the organization while avoiding the possibility of blind spots when devising a strategy. Ultimately, this understanding will position the CSO to successfully tackle the challenges of this increasingly complex world.

CASE STUDY
United Parcel Services (Enabling a Focus on the Bigger Picture)

United Parcel Services (UPS) is an American-based multinational package delivery and supply chain management company. UPS has cargo airlines, freight-based trucking operations, and delivery drones. It is headquartered in Atlanta and has over 481,000 employees worldwide. UPS's revenue in 2018 surpassed $71 billion USD, and the company is a long-time component of the S&P 100 and S&P 500.

WHY AND HOW SCENARIO PLANNING WAS USED

In 1997, UPS was reviewing long-term planning approaches and ultimately chose to bring in a consultancy to assist it in scenario planning workshops. The process used to create the scenarios was as follows:

1. UPS and the consultancy began with workshops based on certain themes, trends, and identified uncertainties.

2. Following workshops, a series of internal and external interviews were conducted that were focused on the main issue of "the future of UPS's global business in an ever-changing competitive environment."

3. Participants of the workshop, predominantly UPS middle and senior managers, went through hours of discussions deciding axes of uncertainty to assist in plotting and producing four scenarios.

4. Teams outlined specific characteristics of each of the scenarios and the position UPS was in, along with its competitors, and identified implications and possible strategies for the corporation.

ORGANIZATIONAL BENEFITS AND RESULTS

In 1999, UPS created the "UPS Charter," which was a guiding document used for the following three years. The charter reflected the change UPS would have to pursue to enable global commerce. The original idea for the charter was sparked from the scenario planning workshops.

The senior management defined themes for UPS's future based on the scenario planning sessions. These themes and scenarios provided a common vocabulary for meetings and within the corporation to conceptualize large ideas.

Numerous executives reported noticing that their teams, as well as themselves, were functioning at a higher level after the workshops because the teams were *connected to the bigger picture of UPS's business model.*

One of the most famous results from scenario planning globally is UPS's acquisition of Mail Boxes Etc. After the scenario planning workshops were completed, senior managers realized how important a retail presence would be for their "prosumers" and further understood that under their "Brave New World" scenario it would be even more important. UPS decided to acquire Mail Boxes Etc. in 2001, which expanded its global retail stores and business services significantly. *Scenario planning resulted in direct strategic action.*[15]

THE ROLE OF THE SCENARIO PLANNERS

The scenario planning team, which typically reports to the chief strategy officer, has the important role of supporting the entire scenario planning process in many organizations. These teams vary considerably by company and have a combination of skills and expertise that enables successful outcomes from both a qualitative and quantitative perspective. Some of the important roles include the following:

- **The Researcher:** The scenario planners support the research of both primary and secondary data that help formulate a picture of future risks and uncertainties in the external world. Researchers need to be able to identify key trends that are of importance to the organization and formulate a sense of critical threats that could disrupt performance and results. Also important are skills in capturing data and information related to political, economic, social, technological, environmental, and legal trends, and the ability to synthesize the information into important observations and insights.

- In practice: The research team should include a combination of economists, policy experts, strategists, and futurists who can bring a mix of qualitative and quantitative skills and expertise to the research approach. In cases where a skill set is missing, other teams within the organization should be used to fill the gap.

- **The Facilitator:** Part of the process of scenario planning is the ability to facilitate important strategic dialogues on the external and internal world and what it means to the organization's strategy. Leadership teams, with the participation of the CEO, need to be brought together to discuss what the information and research has revealed and what it means for the strategy and future options, as well as how risks are going to be mitigated. In some cases, the scenario planners need to be able to facilitate that dialogue, bring strong skills in workshop management, and be able to support conversations among leaders in an effective way. In some cases, CSOs will facilitate the dialogue; in others, they will be participants and the facilitating will be left to the scenario planners.

  - In practice: Facilitators need to be able to create an inclusive environment for a strategic dialogue, stay neutral, keep the energy high, help build alignment and consensus, and manage conflict in a healthy way. They also need to be strong communicators and listeners and able to manage group dynamics.

- **The Presenter:** When scenarios are going to be presented for input and reflection, a lot of material must be prepared before it can be communicated to the audience. The success of the session, including the level of engagement and the dynamic of the group, depends on how the material gets presented. In cases where scenario planners are taking on the role of Presenter, it's important that they bring energy and enthusiasm to the topic, ensure that the information is relevant, provide examples, and really know their subject. It's also important, particularly when leaders and the CEO are involved, to keep it simple, deliver the presentation with impact, and properly prepare for questions that will inevitably arise. Finally, images tell a thousand words and should be used as much as possible to communicate the research that supports the scenarios.

  - In practice: Within the scenario planning team there will be those who have more natural talent as Presenters. They should be chosen to play a central presentation role. It's very important these teams play to their strengths in high-stake strategic conversations.

- **The Writer:** The other skill required when building scenarios is the ability to write and tell a compelling story about potential future realities. Typically, four scenarios are developed as part of the planning process, each telling a different story on a continuum of favourable, neutral, and unfavourable to the organization. The better a story is written, the more likely it will inspire a high degree of engagement and dialogue. It's one thing to gather all the research data and other associated information as part of the exploration and analysis phase but quite another to explain what it all means in a way that will engage others.

- In practice: A well-written scenario told through a story is one that moves us and makes us think, lighting up magnetic impulses in the brain that lead to action. It also becomes something we will remember and take back with us into the organization. It increases empathy in a way that stimulates the brain to have further thoughts and emotions, which is what scenario planning is all about. Finally, powerful scenario
- stories encourage cooperation and help motivate leaders to work with each other.

- **The Coordinator:** The final role of the scenario planner is one of coordination among the different stakeholders involved. The scenario planners need to be able to work across organizational boundaries to gather, analyze, and synthesize information and also support dialogue on the information itself to get alignment on the strategy and on decisions that need to be made. They need to be able to work with finance to get quantitative information, economists to get econometrics, and a variety of internal business units and functions to get information related to internal complexities. They also need to coordinate with external expertise, including consultants, facilitators, and experts who might be presenting on a particular topic. Finally, the Coordinator has an ability to work with the CEO, the executive leadership team, and the CSO.
  - In practice: Someone must quarterback all the work that needs to be done. In some cases, the Coordinator may do some of the work, including research, but also sometimes coordinate with others to do the work and bring it together. Scenario planners need to be able to work within the governance systems of the organization to get things done as efficiently as possible.

CASE STUDY
Anglo American Corporation (Grounding Scenarios in Fundamental Trends and Uncertainties)

Anglo American plc is a South African multinational mining company that is the world's largest producer of platinum and has major production capacity in diamonds, copper nickel alloy, iron ore, and coal. The company has operations on every continent and collects revenue of over $29 billion USD. The company is headquartered in London, United Kingdom, and Johannesburg, South Africa, and employs over 90,000 people worldwide.

WHY AND HOW SCENARIO PLANNING WAS USED

The godfather of scenario planning at Anglo American was Clem Sunter, who is now a world-renowned speaker, scenario planner, and author of many books. In the early 1980s, prior to becoming chairman and CEO of the Gold and Uranium division, he established a scenario planning function at Anglo (with Pierre Wack and Ted Newland, who both had previously headed up scenario planning at Shell). Faced with the combustible circumstances of a country trying to end apartheid, Sunter emphasized the high road of political settlement. The team followed a methodical four-step scenario planning process as part of the desire to better understand risks, uncertainties, and macro driving forces:

1. In 1984, Anglo identified numerous broad global trends, such as the centralization of wealth in certain countries, and a new wave of technological capability.

2. Anglo then defined the rules of the game for "winning nations" where it identified key elements for success in global competition.

3. After identifying key elements for "winning nations," Anglo noted there would be global uncertainties, which were used as the basis for three global scenarios.

4. Anglo, being headquartered in South Africa at the time, then analyzed South Africa's prospects in the context of the global scenario.

5. Lastly, Anglo identified critical domestic uncertainties.

ORGANIZATIONAL BENEFITS AND RESULTS

Based on the scenarios developed, Sunter and his team of Anglo executives were able to *identify early* the risk that South Africa's economic prospects would be low, and they responded by sharing their views and insights with the broader stakeholders on how to embark on a more prosperous future. By doing so, the company was able to engage the wider community on new approaches to risk mitigation.

One of Anglo's scenarios aligned directly with reality when exploring how phasing out the apartheid system would affect the business, allowing the corporation to assess how social demographics could alter their business.

Anglo's scenarios are recognized as successful because they were "intellectually honest, clearly presented, and broad enough to permit a dialogue between opposing power groups." In addition, the scenarios used by Anglo were very dynamic *(fundamentally grounded in trends, uncertainties)*, providing room for healthy internal debate and dialogue.

Using data from the process, Sunter created the much-praised "The World and South Africa in the 1990s" presentation. His work was so influential that he presented it to the country's then-

President, F. W. de Klerk, and his Cabinet as well as to anti-apartheid activist Nelson Mandela, while he was still in prison. Mandela became South Africa's first Black president in 1994.[16]

In summary, it's important to understand the different stakeholders in the system when contemplating scenario planning. By aggregating all the insights, perspectives, influences, and understanding they bring, and connecting all those different views, the scenario planning process will be a success.

Everyone wants to be a problem solver, but most understand that they cannot do it alone. Success is a team effort. The process must be impelled from the top down, and if the CEO does not buy in to the power of the scenario planning process, it cannot be truly successful. The CSO is also crucial in this equation and must act as the provocateur and sponsor of the process, the purveyor of a new way of thinking. Finally, the scenario planners bring the technical expertise that is necessary to coordinate such an important effort.

■ ■ ■

SUMMARY KEY POINTS

- Scenario planning involves a number of key stakeholders to make it successful, from the CEO and CSO to the scenario planners.
- CEOs set the tone from the top. If they have not bought into the process, the organization will not benefit from the power of this management tool. CEOs need to actively engage, hold other leaders accountable, model the right behaviour, and be prepared at times to roll up their sleeves and get involved.

- CEOs own the strategy. Through stress-testing and validating the strategy using scenario planning, the organization has the most to gain in driving the top-down vision.
- The CSO is the most senior strategist in the organization and has an important executive sponsor role in supporting scenario planning. The CSO can help facilitate the process, align senior leaders, and stretch the organization to think more broadly about future realities.
- The CSO is in a unique position to really challenge fellow leaders, including the CEO, to stretch mental models on strategy. The power and importance of this cannot be underestimated.
- Scenario planners make things happen. They conduct research, plan, coordinate, prepare, facilitate, present, and run the process. Different sources of information and activity need to be coordinated and scenario planners ensure this occurs.
- Success in scenario planning is a combination of roles working together to support a process as part of a team effort.

CHAPTER 7

EVOLUTION OF SCENARIO PLANNING USING ARTIFICIAL INTELLIGENCE

"AI is probably the most important thing humanity has ever worked on."

—SUNDAR PICHAI, CEO OF GOOGLE

Although current approaches to scenario planning might work in yesterday's economy, they may not today, not when the only certainty in the future is more change, more uncertainty, more complexity, and an accelerating volume of information. In this world, companies need to adapt to remain competitive. How? If scenario planning is about understanding possible futures, the next natural evolution of this strategic management tool is artificial intelligence, or AI.

In a sense, what I intend to explain is the opposite of the premise of Max Tegmark's influential 2017 book, *Life 3:0: Being Human in the Age of Artificial Intelligence.* Tegmark used scenario planning to develop a number of plausible futures for human beings when AI has become smarter than they are. These possibilities range from humans, cyborgs, and AI peacefully co-existing, to a benevolent AI that allows humans to imagine they're still in control even though they're not, to a super-intelligent and totalitarian AI that decides humans are just a nuisance and destroys them all. My goal is less apocalyptic; I show how humans can extend the utility and value of scenario planning by incorporating AI.

This chapter builds on all the other chapters that provided a solid understanding of the best ways of executing scenario planning. But now we take that baseline to new levels by applying to it the use of AI, which has the potential to expand its future value. This chapter provides several examples of how AI is already being used in scenario planning like analogs and offers insights into new ways humans and machines need to work together on complex strategic processes.

ARTIFICIAL INTELLIGENCE EXPLAINED

So what is AI exactly? For the business world, it's defined as a collection of technologies—including machine learning (ML), natural language processing (NLP), and robotics—that use machines to sense, interpret, and act on data to aid decision-making. It can get confusing because we sometimes see AI, machine learning, deep learning, and big data used as though they're synonymous. There are distinctions, but for the average corporate leader, they're not that important. I use AI as the umbrella term in this chapter.

When it comes to new technologies, there's usually a lot of hype around their capabilities, but with AI the potential risks, opportunities, and benefits are still, if anything, under-hyped. In a March 2019 report, CNBC business reporter Catherine Clifford quoted Bill Gates speaking at the 2019 Human-Centered Artificial Intelligence Symposium at Stanford University. He said: "The world hasn't had that many technologies that are both promising and dangerous—you know, we had nuclear energy and nuclear weapons." Gates went on to say the power of AI is "so incredible, it will change society in some very deep ways."[1]

AI is a classic disruptor: soon it's expected to transform the relationship between people and machines and lead to greater productivity in business. Yet many organizations outside the technology sector have invested proportionally less on digital and AI-related technologies over the last decade. Given the pressures of the modern business world, companies are likely to seek new ways to reduce costs, increase revenues, add capacity and capability, speed up decision-making, and improve quality, while managing risk. AI is often regarded suspiciously, partly because it's seen as risky and unproven, requiring highly skilled programmers and data scientists. But it's also because it requires a sustained, long-term investment of dollars that many companies decide they cannot afford. This reveals a lack of understanding of AI's possibilities—particularly among executives at larger enterprises.

There's another factor involved. Digital fluency and the use of AI technologies have not been seen as core competencies in many organizations that have long been ruled by human operators—namely, mechanical, chemical, and electrical engineers. Early adopters are typically in sectors that are comfortable with technology and have access to standardized data sets.

To be fair, the impact of new technologies is often overestimated in the short term and underestimated in the long term. While there's been a lot of noise regarding AI, there's also been a lack of in-depth discussion and analysis of how it's going to transform businesses. But leaders in organizations that ignore AI advancements and under-invest in it risk being blindsided. AI can allow humans and machines to work together in collectively intelligent ways to support critical business drivers, creating the opportunity to propel organizations into the digital age. It is fast becoming more of a necessity than a luxury.

Whether they're proactive or not, business leaders are aware of this. "AI: Built to Scale," a global study conducted by a team of Accenture researchers led by Ketan Awalegaonkar and released in November 2019, found that 84 percent of C-suite executives believe they must leverage AI

to achieve their growth objectives, yet 76 percent reported they struggle with how to scale this new capability. Furthermore, three out of four
C-suite executives believe that if they don't scale artificial intelligence (AI)
properly in the next five years, they risk going out of business entirely.[2]

STRATEGIC IMPERATIVES FOR THE FUTURE

Successfully deploying AI to help solve strategic problems is built on a few
important drivers and critical questions, which create the backdrop for
any new initiative that would involve this tool.

1. **Costs:** AI won't be successful unless there is a business case—a
   "why" and a link to the bottom-line impact. Given the pressure that
   businesses are under to successfully compete, cost and efficiency need
   to be the vital forces for the strategic success of such transformative
   ways of thinking and developing strategies. Tesla, Inc. has integrated
   a telematics system by which it collects targeted information from
   the engines of its vehicles and processes that data through machine
   learning. In 2014, the company diagnosed components that were
   overheating and "repaired" the vehicles via a software patch. Day to
   day, Tesla can provide predictive maintenance information directly
   to clients, so they're warned of a failure before it happens and are
   given a recommendation for how to address the problem. This saves
   time and potentially more costly repairs down the road.

Here are the questions to be asked:
   - How does the application of AI in a scenario planning context
     integrate into the overall business strategy of operational
     excellence and cost reduction?

- What's the cost-related business case for applying AI?
- What level of cost reduction is required, and where in the business do these opportunities lie?

2. **Quality:** AI needs to be positioned as a tool that enables businesses to make more quality-based strategic decisions and leads to deeper insights and value through the scenario planning process. AI has the potential to assess data and learn from it over time, thus informing different, and perhaps better, decision-making. For example, NASA has been using AI principles to create algorithms that analyze data from the space industry to discover issues before they become serious incidents. "Modern space communications systems use complex software to support science and exploration missions," said Janette C. Briones, principal investigator in the cognitive communication project at NASA Glenn Research Center in Cleveland, Ohio. "By applying artificial intelligence and machine learning, satellites control these systems seamlessly, making real-time decisions without awaiting instruction."[3]

Here are the questions to be asked:
- Have you identified the problems you're trying to solve within the context of scenario planning?
- Do AI tools exist in the business today, and are they being applied successfully to ensure quality outcomes from a strategic perspective?
- Are you willing to invest time and effort into finding the right tool that drives better and more quality-based decisions?

3. **Capabilities:** To drive adoption and uptake, the AI strategy needs to harness the power of humans and machines working together in more collective and intelligent ways in support of scaling the new capability (laying the groundwork to enable and support growth).

There are activities that humans do extremely well and activities that machines do better. The complementary skills and capabilities of both should be used as part of a cultural shift in how work gets done. AI, working in tandem with humans, might be able to more efficiently process data, find correlations, and develop better recommendations on whether to explore and develop a new initiative or to walk away, either creating investment value or saving money. For example, MinePortal, by DataCloud, is a cloud-based AI platform serving the global mining industry. It analyzes geosciences data and provides for real-time management and analysis, allowing mining companies to significantly improve productivity while increasing profitability.

Here are the questions to be asked:

- What activities do humans in the organization do well and not so well?
- Are there opportunities for humans and machines to work together in new and different ways across the scenario planning process?
- Are people willing to trust the technology to help make better decisions and add value?
- What new business capabilities is the organization missing that it wishes it had both now and in the future?

4. **Speed:** Organizations today capture vast amounts of data that teams don't always know how to use or how to process rapidly enough without involving hundreds of people. For AI to be successful, it needs to help organizations use that data in ways it has never been used before—quickly processing vast volumes of information, drawing correlations, learning, and ultimately helping make better

predictions that drive costs down and save time. Goldman Sachs, for example, has developed its own AI tool to analyze resumés with the intent of matching candidates with the division that best fits their experience and career interests. It enables the company to quickly assess thousands of resumés. AI is also shaping the future of stock trading. Analysts forecast markets with greater accuracy and trading firms efficiently mitigate risk and provide higher returns when compared to those that are not fully embracing AI. Robo-advisors analyze millions of data points and execute trades at the optimal price. According to a recent study by the U.K. research firm Coalition, electronic trades represent nearly 45 percent of revenues in cash equities trading. Although hedge funds are more reluctant to embrace automation, many use AI-powered analysts to get investment ideas and build portfolios.

Here are the questions to be asked:

- Does the business capture data today that can be leveraged in an AI context?
- Is the data captured today accurate and quickly accessible?
- Are there opportunities to process and learn from data more quickly?

■ ■ ■

In an October 2018 report, "The Future Workplace: How to Automate Intelligently," from Ernst & Young Global (EY), the researchers studied nearly 2,000 occupations in four economies—the United States, the United Kingdom, Canada, and Australia. Occupations were categorized into 15 business functions and 50 subfunctions across 16 industry sectors. This detailed mapping allowed the EY team to understand how applicable automation was to different economies, sectors, and business functions. One of the findings from this research was that automation has five areas of impact:

1. Fewer workers
2. Scaled capabilities
3. Greater speed
4. Higher quality
5. New capabilities[4]

After leveraging these five areas of impact, leaders need to prioritize the areas that will best help them achieve their business strategy. For example, if lowering the cost of manufacturing production is the goal, automating tasks could result in fewer labourers or a higher quality of output. Alternatively, if increasing the speed of R&D insights is central to the business strategy, then using AI to speed up data gathering, analysis, and decision-making should be prioritized.

In the context of strategic and scenario planning–related processes, organizations suffer from many challenges that prevent them from creating opportunities for improvement using new technologies. An organization's business strategy can indicate a desire to explore and exploit AI, but executing it requires a workplace culture that embraces the new technologies that will, in time, lead to business results.

Washington-based consultant Jean-Francois Orsini was ahead of his time in recognizing the potential of AI to support individual managers and employees and facilitate planning. According to Orsini, planning (including elements of scenario planning) involves formulating an "idealized" future; assessing where that possible future may lie (relying on prediction); assessing the position of the organization within present economic and market conditions; and devising the programs to ensure that, within the required time frame, the organization goes where it wants to go.

In his 1986 paper, "Artificial Intelligence: A Way Through the Strategic Planning Crisis?",[5] he described the many challenges facing strategic planning (of which scenario planning is a sub-component).

1. The alienating behaviour of the strategic planning staff
2. The demands of the planning staff
3. The wrong predictions made by planners
4. The division created by planners between top management and line managers
5. The demands of the planning process
6. The impediment created by the planning process in adequately assessing the outside world
7. The rigidity of plans and their dangerous consequences
8. The simplistic nature of plans that makes corporate moves transparent to the competition and increases its vulnerability
9. Inadequate contingency plans
10. The difficulty of implementing plans

When I look at the ten challenges he outlined, I would draw particular attention to certain ones: number 2 (demands on planning staff), 3 (wrong predictions), 5 (demands of the planning process), 6 (outside world), 7 (rigid plans), and 9 (contingency plans). I think that AI applied to scenario planning can help with many of these specific challenges.

The challenges are even more present today than when Orsini wrote his report, creating an opportunity to consider better ways to approach the process. Orsini believes planning is part art and part science and you should not overemphasize the tools. However, given the volume of information that needs to be scanned and the complex relationships that need to be understood in scenario planning today, the potential of using an AI-based tool to help reduce costs, improve quality, speed up results, and enhance capabilities should not be underestimated. No, you will never eliminate challenges, like incorrect predictions about the future based on poor-quality data, and there are always going to be aspects of the process that require human oversight, but other actions, involving data-crunching, for example, lend themselves to AI-related tools.

BIG DATA AND DECISION-MAKING

The use of AI has led to dramatic improvements in how large amounts of data can be analyzed to make better and faster decisions in a variety of areas. Gartner Inc's 2018 Technology Trends Survey[6] listed AI as the number-one strategic technology, partly because it enhances decision-making, but also because it reinvents business models and ecosystems.

Approximately every 10 years, there is a substantial development in the AI space, and looking back it started with the development of decision support systems (1980s), then data warehousing (1990s), followed by real-time data warehousing (2000s), and big data analytics (2010s). The next development, due in the early 2020s, will be about the increasing sophistication of AI, reports Hugh J. Watson, a professor of Management Information Systems at the University of Georgia, in his 2017 paper, "Preparing for the Cognitive Generation of Decision Support."[7] By moving data to the cloud and harnessing sensors, streaming data, and the Internet of Things (IoT), AI will become more pervasive within organizations as machines become increasingly human-like in their intelligence.

Although not every organization may be at the stage where it is ready to build AI applications, at a minimum leaders should be planning on a future where data will be used to power smart solutions. Perhaps the single most important detail to remember is that the results of AI solutions are only as good as the quality of the data. It's also important to remember that right now the world has more data than it knows what to do with, so the winners will be the organizations that find smart ways to use these large quantities of data to produce insights as to what the future risks, trends, uncertainties, and drivers might be.

WHAT CAN AI DO TODAY?

We can all see how AI is deployed in systems that address higher volume and lower value decisions. For example, Amazon or Netflix use AI to suggest purchases for their subscribers. ("If you liked this book or movie, you may also like these.")

Here's another use. By combining big data and AI, the technology has the power to allow data from news media and social media to be quickly processed, absorbing insights and trends with a processing power far superior to humans. Given that 90 percent of all the data in the world has been created in the last two years, it's not the volume you collect but your ability to process and assess important insights from this data that will give your organization a competitive edge. According to a 2019 study by Ashley DiFranza, a marketing and content media specialist at Northeastern University, many organizations have embraced the use of data, but they are only scratching the surface of its potential. Many organizational decision-makers are unaware of analytical advances that allow them to make predictive, rather than descriptive, use of their collected data, and those that are aware of it may not have the technical understanding to fully appreciate the potential of this change.[8]

Snorkel.org, an open-source program developed at Stanford University, is an example of a sophisticated new data-processing tool that helps label and organize data sets. Its goal: to explore the radical idea that it's possible to bring mathematical precision to the messy, often entirely manual process of the creation and management of "training data," the information that helps programs learn how to intelligently perform tasks training. Beginning in 2019, Snorkel has been building a platform to support this vision: Snorkel Flow, an end-to-end machine-learning platform for developing and deploying AI applications. One of the biggest obstacles to scenario planning is exploring the outside world to identify risks, trends, uncertainties, and threats. The data comes in many different forms and can be very messy, making it hard for planners to process it and glean important insights. Snorkel can help with the labelling, organizing, structuring, and processing. For business, it represents machine learning in a form that is faster, more flexible, and more practical than ever before.

In cases where rules can be applied, AI can be very powerful. It is good at reasoning based on analogies and it can retrieve information after calculating the most closely related example to a situation in order to help implement similar strategies. So, for example, if AI found a pattern that occurred for a competitive company (a market driver, for example, that forced the competitor out of business), it could highlight that driver and alert leaders to a risk.

There has also been the development of what is called "fuzzy systems," which allow the user to get further analysis by inputting information that is not quantified. Fuzzy logic (FL) is based on the human method of reasoning that involves all the intermediate possibilities between what is true and false. It is able to recognize, interpret, and make use of, as humans can, data that is vague and imprecise. This is often the kind of input one encounters in scenario planning, so there is great potential for this application in the future.

AI can potentially help scenario planning in other ways too:

- Natural language processing (NLP) is a branch of AI that involves the reading and understanding of spoken or written language through the medium of a computer. This includes the automatic translation of one language into another but also the automatic answering of questions. For example, Siri uses a variety of advanced machine learning technologies, including NLP, to understand commands and provide responses. NLP can be used to process information on the Internet, such as corporate reports, news articles, Twitter feeds, Facebook posts, and other data sources, and identify risks, threats, opportunities, and more as part of scenario planning.

- Bayesian networks are statistical models that take an event and predict the likelihood that one of several possible known causes was the contributing factor. They are used for a variety of tasks, including prediction, anomaly detection, diagnostics, and decision-making when faced with uncertainty. They are often used in medical applications to look at symptoms and compute the probability of various diseases. Given this ability, Bayesian networks could be perfectly suited to scenario planning, which also deals with a range of probabilities and possible outcomes.

- A neural network is a series of algorithms that mimics the way the human brain works, with limitless potential to solve new problems. Although no one knows where this field will go in the future, if scenario planning is about thinking strategically and understanding what to do based on different future realities, advancements in neural networks could be the next evolution of strategic thinking. Imagine asking a machine to process data feeds and provide possible answers with supporting information.

HOWEVER, THERE ARE STILL LIMITATIONS

"Wicked" problems in business are the hardest to solve, and strategic decisions often fall into this category. They are fuzzy, complex, unstructured, ambiguous, and difficult to formulate, and the more you try to tame them the more complicated they become. For this kind of problem, AI doesn't help much, according to a 1991 paper by William E. Spangler, dean and professor of Management at Pittsburgh's Duquesne University.[9] The specific issue with scenario planning is that it involves communication and negotiation with other individuals in the organizational decision-making process. Executives, especially, tend to resist the use of computer-based systems to make decisions because strategy is viewed as a highly creative and intuitive process. For scenario planning purposes, data scientists need to understand that leaders respond to storytelling and the story must be plausible (containing enough familiar elements to ground the scenario in reality).

For now, AI can be used only to augment human decision-making, not replace it, because it cannot explain the reasoning process—why a decision was made a certain way. In addition, humans learn over time, through experience and experimentation, to make better decisions. Gradually, AI systems are learning to do the same. When thinking about the potential application of AI to processes like scenario planning, it's important to clearly understand the extent to which it can replace, rather than enhance, the process, including the subtle shifts in decision-making, both big and strategic, small and tactical, that happen along the way. When it comes to decisions involved in scenario planning, for now AI is at its best when playing a supporting role; with future developments this may change.

It's important not to dismiss more strategic applications of AI too quickly, because the technology is constantly maturing and evolving as scientists and tech companies invest billions of dollars in research and development to correct its strategic limitations. Success will be achieved when ways are found for humans and machines to work together on different parts of the process.

HUMANS AND AI CAN WORK TOGETHER

Some experts, like Accenture senior executives H. James Wilson and Paul R. Daugherty in their 2018 *Harvard Business Review* article, "Collaborative Intelligence: Humans and AI Are Joining Forces,"[10] believe that AI is having the greatest impact when it enhances, rather than replaces, human activity. Collective intelligence occurs when AI and humans come together with different, but complementary, skills: AI has the scalability (the ability to grow and expand) and the quantitative power to process vast amounts of data, with humans providing the teamwork and creative skills. Probably the most common example of collective intelligence is how millions of people across the planet create web pages on the Internet; Google's technology searches all that information and, in seconds, produces intelligent results.

In another influential study, "Organizational Decision-Making Structures in the Age of AI,"[11] a team of researchers led by Dr. Yash Raj Shrestha, chair of strategic management and innovation at ETH Zurich, explored the different ways human and AI-based decision-making can work. Based on a comparison of human and AI-based decision-making, the article presents four ways that humans and machines can work together:

1. Full human-to-AI delegation, where AI-based algorithms make decisions without human intervention (for example, high-frequency trading, fraud detection, or dynamic pricing on Airbnb)

2. AI-to-human sequential decision-making, where AI does an initial screening and then humans take over (for example, in recruitment and hiring, AI reviews hundreds of resumés and makes a short list; humans make a decision on the final offer)

3. Hybrid human-to-AI decision-making (for example, health monitoring and sports analytics; the Oakland Athletics baseball team uses humans to select a short list of players to draft and then uses AI to make the final selection)

4. Aggregated human-AI decision-making (for example, used with top management teams and boards where human and AI decision-making are combined independently. For years, BMW used the old system of an assembly line of workers with industrial robots relegated to a corner of the factory; when the company brought human workers and robots together to collaborate, the result was about 85 percent more productive)

In summary, machines and humans working together ("collective intelligence") take on different forms depending on the need.

FASTER, BETTER

AI tools have the potential to help organizations find ways to strengthen the existing workforce, causing better and faster decision-making, and analyzing at great speed the huge amounts of data required to glean insights in game-changing ways. SEB, a major Swedish bank, is using a virtual assistant called Aida to interface with millions of customers 24/7. The assistant handles various questions on typical banking processes, but whenever the system cannot answer a question, it transitions the call to a human who handles the more complex issues.[12]

Humans assist machines by explaining the data gathered through external analysis, ensuring the AI machines are correctly set up and focused on the right information, and training the systems using algorithms. In his 2018 paper, "Artificial Intelligence and the Future of Work: Human-AI Symbiosis in Organizational Decision Making,"[13] Mohammad Hossein Jarrahi, a professor at the University of North Carolina's School of Information and Library Science, highlights the complementary nature of humans and machines. While machines have impressive analytical powers, "much of cognition and human decision making is not a direct result of deliberate information gathering and processing, but instead arises from the subconscious in the realm of intuition.... Superior intuition can be understood as a gut feeling or business instinct about the outcome of an investment or new product." Humans have this ability to deal with uncertainty by making swift, intuitive decisions in the face of the unknown but can be supported by real-time information provided by AI. Furthermore, when tackling complexity, humans decide where to seek and gather data, choosing among options and leveraging AI to collect, process, and analyze the data.

The challenge for the C-suite will be to find approaches to quickly realign businesses to fully take advantage of the knowledge they're learning from AI technologies. Building the organizational infrastructure and models to enable AI to work takes strong leadership, long-term effort, a willingness to fail, and the ability to rethink how the organization has done things in the past. Leaders today have the opportunity to stay ahead of their competitors by adopting a rigorous approach to identifying and prioritizing AI-related projects that build distinctive market advantages and deliver value for their businesses. The potential advantages, if managed carefully and responsibly, are limitless.

CASE STUDY
Port of Rotterdam and Utrecht University
(Understanding Market Potential)

The Port of Rotterdam is Europe's largest seaport, known for its ability to transport petrochemicals and other general cargo. Renowned for its outstanding accessibility for sea-going vessels, it was the world's busiest port from 1962 until 2004, when Singapore and Shanghai surpassed it. The Port of Rotterdam is operated by the Port of Rotterdam Authority, which is governed by the municipality of Rotterdam and the Dutch state.

WHY AND HOW SCENARIO PLANNING WAS USED

The Port of Rotterdam wanted to stimulate the development of a "biomass hub concept" (biomass is plant or animal material used for clean energy production or in various other industrial processes). It hired Utrecht University to conduct a study to "quantify potential trade flows used for heat and electricity generation in the captive and contestable hinterland of Rotterdam to 2030."

The university first developed scenarios based on model projections and biomass resource assessments. Resource assessments included global biomass supply, geographically specific cost-supply curves of biomass, biomass export regions, FOB prices, important facilities such as seaports, and uncertainties that policy makers and utilities are facing. The study focused on both supply and demand in order to understand the trade flow and resulting implications.

The university's team then dove into the scenarios and described the data and background in further detail for each one. The team also reviewed an assessment of biomass supply potentials and demand of biomass with updated information to better inform the scenarios and strengthen their accuracy.

ORGANIZATIONAL BENEFITS AND RESULTS

The Port of Rotterdam "aims to handle 9-10 million tones of biomass in 2020" and the report, published by Utrecht University, outlined three different scenarios (with supply and demand data). These scenarios assisted the port in understanding the market potential, the nuances of supply and demand in the region, and potential dynamics that should be monitored.

With the study in hand, Port of Rotterdam management had a much clearer understanding of the pivotal role the port would play in the future of biomass in the region and was able to capitalize on it. The work enhanced the organization's ability to foresee multiple futures and manage uncertainty.[14]

STRATEGIC FORESIGHT AND HORIZON SCANNING

Strategic foresight is the ability to identify drivers of change and prepare for multiple plausible future outcomes, writes engineer and AI scientist Tamal Chowdhury in a 2019 LinkedIn post.[15] It is not about predicting the future but trying to understand how different versions of the future might play out—understanding the multiple realities in a scenario planning–type way. Chowdhury talks about strategic foresight—similar to scenario planning, which is focused on helping organizations manage risk—as channelling risks in a way that creates competitive advantage and supports the strategic objectives of an organization. He also claims that many organizations miss important external signals, or signposts, and, perhaps, with better scenario planning and strategic processes enabled by AI, these organizations could have avoided negative outcomes.

For example, during the first three quarters of 2019, Amazon Web Services (AWS) and Microsoft's Azure dominated the public cloud with market shares of 39 percent and 19 percent, respectively, according to records kept by Statista. IBM was a distant sixth, with only a 3 percent share. When it comes to the public cloud, IBM is neither biggest nor best. Not only did IBM give AWS seven years to dominate hardware sales before fitfully responding, it also failed to invest enough to ensure that it would have best-in-class enterprise products.

Meanwhile, BlackBerry was the producer of the world's first, widely adopted premium smartphone brand. At its peak, BlackBerry owned more than a 50 percent share of the U.S. smartphone market, and 20 percent of the global market. The dominant brand through 2010, the "CrackBerry," so named because of the addictive hold it had over its owners, sold more than 50 million devices a year and boasted a stock price of over $230 a share. Today, BlackBerry has 0 percent share of the smartphone market and its stock price has hovered in the high single digits for most of the past few years. How could this happen? Clearly its leaders reacted too slowly to market changes, focused on the wrong end market, misunderstood the smartphone's value proposition, and was characterized by generally poor execution.

Had the company properly used scenario planning, it could have anticipated that consumers—not business customers—would drive the smartphone revolution and recognized that users preferred touchscreens to keyboards. Knowing this, its management might have made different investments in innovation, acquisitions of tech companies, and hiring decisions. AI could have enhanced the scenario planning process because of its ability to assess risks and threats as well as identify trends and shifts in consumer behaviour beyond human computational power.

The challenge with traditional scenario planning processes is that they are very hands-on, involving strategic planners, executives, and other stakeholders working together in workshops and meetings, executing a process that takes time and sucks up valuable resources. A lot of the data analysis and research is performed manually by humans poring over documents, websites, reports, and other documentation and analyzing the information. The problem is that things get missed, and the ability to monitor information in real time is too difficult. This is where horizon scanning using AI could be exploited, according to Chowdhury, enabling organizations to anticipate emerging issues, risks, and trends, including those that are on the margins of current thought.

Strategic foresight almost always includes a horizon scanning phase. Horizon scanning involves processing and assessing huge amounts of data, including websites, social media, conventional news sources, and more, a task that would be impossible for humans to do alone. The objective of horizon scanning is to identify developments—risks, threats, trends, persistent issues—that might change or disrupt a company's plans for the future. "Scanning the horizon" could turn up a new and competitive technology, an economic restructuring, a global conflict, a pandemic, a shift in gender roles or societal values. The possibilities are endless, and this kind of information provides valuable insights that may influence scenario planning decisions.

In the context of scenario planning, the ability to monitor outliers or potential market shocks becomes a very important strategy for organizations to master. There are AI tools that can help the horizon scanning process do just that. Sentiment analysis, for example, involves analyzing views—whether positive, negative, or neutral—from written text to gauge reactions. Opinion mining is the use of computational linguistics, text analytics, and natural language processing to identify and extract information from source materials. It can, for example, allow businesses to identify customer attitudes toward a product, service, or brand in online feedback. In addition, unsupervised learning and reinforcement learning offer scalable ways to develop multiple versions of the future. So different AI technologies can help organizations make sense of all kinds of data that feed into scenario planning.

In summary, using AI to scan the horizons, process data, look for patterns, and assess and uncover potential connections, as well as potential risks, are all examples of where AI can augment the human processes involved in scenario planning and strategic planning. This does not remove the need to digest the results and communicate and engage within the organization while ultimately making decisions based on the data, but it offers a window into how humans and AI can work together to make sense of an increasingly complex and uncertain world.

CASE STUDY
Royal Dutch Shell (Creating an Early Warning System)

Royal Dutch Shell, commonly known as Shell, is a Dutch-British oil and gas company with headquarters in the Netherlands and England. Shell was ranked as the ninth-largest company in the world (and the largest outside of China and the United States), and the world's largest energy company in 2019. Vertically integrated in the oil and gas industry with operations across the globe, Shell employs more than 82,000 people.

WHY AND HOW SCENARIO PLANNING WAS USED

Shell is the pioneer of scenario planning, having been using it since the 1970s. Before scenario planning, the company used a UPM (Unified Planning Machinery) system, which forecasted six years ahead and was often ineffective. With UPM showing challenges with productivity, the company began testing scenario planning and further developed it with groundbreaking results. The following process is how, in 1972, scenario planning was used by the organization for the first time:

1. The scenario team would develop broad scenarios.
2. Scenarios would be reviewed and "structured" in order to assist managers and executives to understand the uncertainties and "come to grips with them."
3. Further investigation into the "principal actors in Shell's business environment were analysed," such as their producers, consumers, and competitors.
4. After gaining a greater understanding of the system, Shell's scenario team revamped the scenarios and clustered them into families.
5. From the family of scenarios, the teams at Shell would propose potential solutions to each family of scenarios. This "family of scenarios" model provided a wide enough scope for the organization to assess numerous uncertainties at once, mirroring a more realistic challenge.

ORGANIZATIONAL BENEFITS AND RESULTS

Based on the scenarios, Shell's scenario planners were able to warn their upstream managers in advance to be careful about losing major parts of their concession and mining rents, as the host nations to the oil and gas industry were becoming unstable and drastically changing their policies. In addition, scenario planners were able to warn Shell's downstream refiners to anticipate periods of low growth as the demand for oil, which had been growing more rapidly than GDP, was expected to level off in the 1970s as industrial countries became more efficient. This intelligence from planners enabled leaders of the firm's business units to strategically pivot before these macro events could negatively impact the business.

Another outcome from the scenario planning exercise of 1972 was that Shell began decentralizing its decision-making process. Prior to that year, Shell was run as a global company and did not apply the level of strategy required to succeed in specific areas of the world. Instead, Shell adopted a successful country-specific strategic approach that its leaders recognized from the scenarios.

Today the company employs a full-time team of scenario planners to constantly explore and help the wider organization. Their findings enable the firm's leaders to undertake complex decision-making to exploit the future. Shell's scenarios ask "What if?" questions, encouraging leaders to consider events that may only be remote possibilities but that stretch their mental models. Furthermore, Shell's scenarios help governments, academia, and business in understanding possibilities and uncertainties ahead. Shell strives to ensure its scenarios are plausible and challenging descriptions of the future landscape. They have helped Shell make complex decisions in times of uncertainty and grapple with tough energy and environmental issues.[16]

STRATEGIC APPLICATIONS OF AI

The following examples represent just a few current applications of AI in the strategic planning space.

- **Risk:** There are several emerging examples of AI being applied to strategic-related decision-making processes. A well-established one is in the risk management space, as Saqib Aziz and Michael Dowling, from the Rennes School of Business in France, wrote in a 2018 paper, "AI and Machine Learning for Risk Management."[17] For example, AI supports market traders on risks related to trading positions by detecting fraud, improving compliance, and reducing model risk. Aziz and Dowling point to the credit software firm, Zest AI, which evaluates large volumes of data on customers, such as purchasing histories, to make important decisions about lending using thousands of data points per customer. Such data would be difficult and time-consuming for humans to process, but AI is able to make decisions within seconds using clustering and decision trees as well as deep learning capabilities. In 2017 the company saw a 150 percent increase in lending with no change in credit losses. In the credit risk space, Aziz and Dowling found evidence that AI can significantly increase credit risk management capabilities by helping collect and make sense of all the complex, unstructured data.

  In the financial investment sector, there is significant exposure to external financial markets. Working closely with human experts, AI can help with data preparation, modelling, stress-testing, and validating future models. This avoids the risk that the model is wrong, but also stress-tests the market models for risk. For example, Yields.io is a financial tech company serving a portfolio of clients made up of investment banks, insurance companies, and other financial institutions. Supported by AI, its platform helps C-level executives identify critical areas of model risk across the enterprise.

- **Regulatory:** One further example explored by Aziz and Dowling with an interesting application to the scenario planning world relates to the regulatory system. With increasing external demands to remain compliant, AI can help with large volumes of data that need to be assessed with real-time monitoring capabilities to prevent compliance breaches. IBM, for example, purchased Promontory, a regulatory technology start-up that offers services to reduce the cost of compliance. This real-time monitoring of regulatory-related risks has the power to transform the external risk detection and response processes. It ensures that a firm is following what is usually, in most sectors, a highly complex regulatory environment, one that usually represents common and time-consuming strategic discussions at the management table. Finding new ways to predict and manage risk could add tremendous value.

- **Scenario Planning Advisor:** The evaluation of external risks is an important aspect of scenario planning, but the really interesting potential of AI lies in using the external information to develop future realities or scenarios. IBM has developed a tool called Scenario Planning Advisor (SPA) that takes external news information and generates scenarios through a decision support system, as detailed in a 2018 paper written by a team led by Shirin Sohrabi, research manager of AI Planning and Applications at IBM's Watson Research Center in New York.[18] Each scenario highlights the potential leading indicators (the set of facts that lead to the scenario), the scenario itself, and the emerging risks that, when combined, explain the consequences of the scenario, including the business implications. Although SPA is in the pilot stage, it has the power to go beyond purely external risk management and the identification of risks for consideration, and into the world of scenario development and interpretation.

The SPA system works by continuously monitoring news and social media information that is relevant to an organization, factors in the risk drivers for the specific business (domain) sector, and applies reasoning to the incomplete and potentially biased raw data. Then it generates a set of scenarios used to support the strategic conversations. Through its three architectural components—the planning engine that generates three to six scenarios, the news aggregator that deals with the raw data from the news using text analysis, and the domain knowledge system—SPA has the power to transform how scenario planning will be practised in the future.

- **War Games:** Another example of the strategic application of AI is the U.S. Army, which is in a continuous cycle of research and development as the country looks to maintain its global position and operational superiority. In 2000, a team of researchers, led by Austin Tate, professor of knowledge-based systems in the School of Informatics at the University of Edinburgh, explored the use of AI specifically for strategic planning in small unit operations, providing a rare example of AI being used across the full planning cycle.[19] The AI technology was able to support a force carrying out a mission in an extreme urban setting where leaders could face unexpected and dangerous situations requiring instantaneous decision-making. The planning involved pre-mission preparation, adjusting the plan en route to the target when necessary, and rapid decision-making when conditions changed during life-or-death moments of combat. These elements have parallels with the scenario planning process in bringing knowledge forward, considering options before making strategic decisions, and handling dynamic risks and issues as they evolve. Similar to the objectives of scenario planning, the application ultimately provides great situational awareness of the uncertainties of the external environment.

- **Weather:** One final example of the application of AI in helping with strategic decision-making and external monitoring of risks and uncertainties relates to high-impact weather, such as severe thunderstorms, hurricanes, and tornados, which caused $7.9 billion in property damage in the United States in 2015. The variety and volume of data associated with weather forecasting can be overwhelming, so using AI can improve the accuracy of predictions and help handle the large number of unpredictable variables, integrating a physical understanding of the environment into those variables. Using decision trees popular for handling big data like this, Amy McGovern, from the School of Computer Science at the University of Oklahoma, and a team of researchers tested machine learning and the prediction of storm duration. Using AI, the system was able to rapidly filter through the data, extract the insights, and provide accurate and timely guidance to human weather forecasters and decision-makers.[20]

Many more examples exist and more will continue to emerge as the technology matures and evolves. For scenario planners, AI represents an exciting opportunity to drive costs down, improve speed and quality, and enhance planning capabilities.

CRITICAL SUCCESS FACTORS TO USING AI IN SCENARIO PLANNING

When thinking about the deployment of AI in the context of scenario planning, it's important not only to identify the potential scenario planning processes where AI can be applied in the end-to-end sequence of activities but also to understand broader considerations related to leadership, strategy, roles and responsibilities, data, platforms, governance, and capabilities. These all play a role in successfully adopting AI-driven scenario planning within an organization.

Outlined in this section is a set of critical success factors that will help support the process of adopting AI to scenario planning:

- **Leadership engagement:** Buy-in and support are required at the C-suite level. AI projects require a fundamental shift in how work gets done and how decisions are made, as well as an ongoing effort to build and refine models and help the tools learn. So support from the top is necessary to ensure adequate investment and to manage the transformation. Leaders at the top don't need to understand the technology, but they do need to support the organization's experimentation and the business case for AI. This is especially true in helping management understand the outputs, because they will be initially hesitant to base decisions and careers on a system and models that they don't completely understand. Hugh Watson, in his 2017 paper, highlighted the importance of a new role called the "model and data interpreter, an individual who helps communicate the analytics and business intelligence outputs in a storytelling way that the organization's leaders can understand."[21]

- **Strategic integration:** Any AI activity that might be planned as part of a long-term effort, including aspects of cost reduction, needs to be tightly integrated into the business strategy. AI should also be integrated into the digital/IT strategy as well as across the entire organization's silos. To be successful, it has to be a team effort and cross functionally supported.

- **Long-term thinking:** AI is not a one-and-done program but an ongoing capability that needs to be developed in the organization, either through insourcing or outsourcing, as part of a digital ecosystem. Organizations that want to drive value in AI deployment need to consider the multiple horizons and appreciate the ongoing effort and patience required for success. There is no silver bullet to make AI work; it will inevitably require collaborating with partners, refining models, and testing. Many early projects will have a low return on investment and a limited impact—they will primarily function as learning opportunities—but that learning is the first step on a transformational journey. In addition, as part of the long-term thinking, it's important to consider the broader cognitive architecture. If the organization wants to generate an understanding of what the future will look like using AI-driven scenario planning, it cannot do it based on today's technologies and human capabilities.

- **Problem definition and types:** AI works best when problems can be broken down into many unambiguously binary decisions—A or B. (Is the emerging technology a threat or not? Will the competitor succeed or fail? Are interest rates going to go up or down?) The number of binary decisions can grow over time, and AI can pick the right path for every binary decision, but business leaders need to be sure they've selected a problem that is the kind best suited for AI to successfully solve. Finally, pilot projects can help generate momentum and prove the technology works, so using these can accelerate the long-range journey.

- **Phased approach:** It is crucial to think about the business approach to AI in a structured and methodical way.
  - Defining the business problem you're trying to solve

- Collecting the data (for example, using sensors), which in many cases companies already do

- The prediction. This is where the magic happens. Having agreed on a problem to be solved, AI processes the data, the algorithms run their course, and the results are presented; they will, in some cases, result in a prediction that the team can assess.

- **Organizational capabilities:** It seems obvious that in order to deploy AI, you'll need human skills in programming, mathematics, and deep IT areas such as architecture to help design and deploy the tools. (IT architecture is a series of principles, guidelines, or rules used by an enterprise to direct the process of acquiring, building, modifying, and interfacing IT resources throughout the enterprise.) But perhaps what's less clear is the need for someone to interpret the tests that result from humans and machines working together. In addition, the role that engineers can play as translators to the quantitative analysts ("quants") who are doing the deep analysis and building models is critical to success. Humans need to step in when the machine fails, which is also an opportunity for the machine to learn from the human. At an enterprise level, it's also important to strategically assess the capabilities you build within an organization and those that you outsource to third parties, and to consider how the workforce needs to transform the way it works in the future.

  Think about collaborating with all kinds of organizations and third parties as part of building a wider ecosystem. Organizations have historically wanted to amass all their talent in-house, but the future of work today needs to be a more hybrid approach where some work is done internally and the rest is farmed out to external partners. For example, the profile of a data scientist is someone who is a math and computer whiz with highly evolved trend-spotting skills and the ability to extract intelligence from large data sets and solve complex problems. It's hard to recruit this kind of talent from the relatively small, highly specialized field of data science, but a recent IBM study[22] predicted that business will need 28 percent more data scientists worldwide to cope with an increasing demand, thanks to companies, large and small, embracing big data to improve decision-making. Fayrix, an Israeli software development company, permits organizations to outsource its data scientists, on long- or short-term contracts, to fill their needs. "Outsourcing data science is the future because it's the only way to use the latest technologies in the most reliable and efficient manner," said Ofer Zvi, Fayrix's director.[23] This at a time when the United States could have a need for as many as 250,000 data scientists by 2024. It's also important, of course, to be creative in meeting the staffing needs and always look to hire the smartest people you can.

- **Foundational data:** Organizations are flush with data, but getting the right data, cleaning it up, and making it accessible is a critically important step. This involves having appropriate risk monitoring and management in place. Like humans, machines will struggle to process poor data. To ensure the results are unbiased, be sure the machine is fed data relating to projects that have both failed and succeeded, so its learning is balanced. Finally, having the processing power that can handle the volumes of data to feed to the machine is a potential gap at some companies and may require additional investment.

- **Platform selection:** AI involves large amounts of mathematics (statistical formulas) on top of decision trees. Each statistical formula is different depending on the problem you're solving. The technology platforms need to support the calculations (different platforms use different mathematics) and support a continuous AI learning loop. It's also important to decide whether the platform is for an early experiment, to see whether things are working, or is intended to be scaled across the company for long-term use. The world of AI is so new that the platform might not exist next year, so it's critical to record your code so that you can use it on another platform in the future.

- **Technology differences:** It's important to make sure you understand the difference between machine learning (ML), which is based on algorithms that can learn from data, and more traditional rules-based programming, including robotic process automation (RPA), which is a software robot that performs repetitive tasks while following strict rules. The latter is like a clerk who is good at clerical work but will never ascend into upper management. Both play a role in business, so it's critical to be clear about the differences and when and how to apply them.

- **Overcome the fear factor:** The media tends to focus on the fears associated with AI rather than the benefits, so leaders at large enterprises may spend more bandwidth addressing those fears than exploring the opportunities. The AI community needs to take ownership of this issue and encourage conversations that allow business leaders to address and move past their legitimate concerns. Within AI, which is simply a continuum of the technology revolution, there are two main types: specialized and general. We see specialized AI all around us: Siri, facial recognition, Snapchat filters, Amazon recommendations, Nest thermostats, and many more. Artificial general intelligence is the hypothetical intelligence of a machine that has the capacity to understand or learn any intellectual task that a human being can. It is a primary goal of some AI research and is a common topic in science fiction and future studies. As we advance this general intelligence component of AI, we must be very careful to ensure we protect humans and develop the technology in a responsible and ethical way.

EXTENDING THE VALUE CURVE

Uncertainty and complexity are always present. There are many steps involved in producing a robust scenario plan as part of a wider strategic planning process—engagement among stakeholders, research, dialogue with leaders, tinkering as gaps are identified, etc. The scenario planning process is further complicated by the need to consider scenarios that involve an ever-changing external environment. The challenge facing both the strategic planner and chief strategic officer is how to drive value at the speed, cost, quality, and capability required. This is where AI can help.

By using AI as a programming, data-gathering, and mathematics tool, some of these challenges can be overcome. As an example, DeepMind Technologies, creator of the gaming program, AlphaStar, is exploring new and exciting ways of using AI to help solve some of the world's most real-life problems. The DeepMind team's approach is to apply game theory and deep neural networks to real-time strategy problems burdened with imperfect information, notes Daniel Shapiro, cofounder and chief technology officer of Designlab, an online educational platform, in a 2019 article in *Forbes*.[24] This new system operates on a combination of supervised and reinforced learning, and what makes it unique is its ability to work with incomplete information. The technology will have a huge impact on the financial sector, Shapiro writes, "where 80 percent of market activity is algorithmic trading agents, and automated strategy plays a major role in these agents moving markets."

Big data, analytics, and AI are providing transformative capabilities within organizations to predict the future based on the past. These powerful tools, demonstrated by several examples in this chapter, will help companies compete in an ever-changing business environment. As outlined in the Ernst and Young (EY) 2014 report, "Big Data: Changing the Way Businesses Compete and Operate,"[25] the idea of data creating business value is not new; however, the use of data is becoming the basis of competitive advantage. "Big data will fundamentally change the way businesses compete and operate," wrote EY's global risk leader, Paul van Kessel, in the report. "Companies that invest in and successfully derive value from their data will have a distinct advantage over their competitors—a performance gap that will continue to grow as more relevant data is generated, emerging technologies and digital channels offer better acquisition and delivery mechanisms, and the technologies that enable faster, easier data analysis continue to develop." The report also indicates that while the ability for AI to capture and store vast amounts of data has grown at an unprecedented rate, the technical capacity to aggregate and analyze these stockpiles of information is only now catching up.

In the future, scenario planning enabled by AI will play a very important role in optimizing the processing power of organizations. AI will create new and more insightful models to deal with external forces, support strategic decisions in real-time, and offer newer and better internal and external applications to predict and create value. Whether by using IBM's SPA tool or some in-house customized AI model, organizations will continue to develop new ways to make sense of information; build patterns, insights, and observations that inform strategy; and ultimately make better, more informed decisions based on the data.

In summary, the good news is that humans won't be replaced in the scenario planning process, but fusion skills will emerge; these are skills where AI and humans work together in a more integrated way, enhancing the overall capability of the enterprise and producing better outcomes than either could achieve alone. As Andrew Hill pointed out in a 2019 *Financial Times* article, "The human strategist is still required, precisely to decide when and why to deviate from the strategy framework, whether that frame is built by a committee of people or a highly intelligent machine."[26]

■ ■ ■

SUMMARY KEY POINTS

- AI is a collection of technologies, including machine learning, deep learning, big data, natural language processing (NLP), and robotics, that allow machines to aid decision-making by sensing, interpreting, learning, and acting upon information.

- AI will disrupt and transform the relationship between people and machines and drive greater productivity in businesses. Success will be based on finding new and better ways for machines and humans to work together.

- Success in the deployment of AI to help solve strategic problems, such as scenario planning, is predicated on a few important drivers, such as cost, quality, capability, and speed. Leaders need to prioritize which area will best support achievement of the business strategy and outcomes.

- Many challenges exist today in current strategic planning and scenario planning processes, including alienation of staff, wrong predictions about the future, and limited data-processing power. Planning outcomes can be rigid. Assessing the risks, trends, uncertainties, and threats of the outside world can be overwhelming and complicated. But they are all opportunities that the application of AI may help identify.

- The use of AI has enabled dramatic improvements in how large amounts of data can be analyzed to make better and faster decisions, based on new and often startling insights.

- The challenge with strategic decisions compared to tactical decisions is that the former are fuzzy, complex, unstructured, ambiguous, and difficult to formulate. That makes them difficult to apply to a tool like AI. It's important to select the aspects of scenario planning that lend themselves to AI-based solutions.

- Combining big data and AI together has the exciting potential to allow data from, say, news media and social media, to be processed quickly and their insights and trends revealed at a processing speed superior to humans.

- Strategic foresight is the ability to identify drivers of change and prepare for multiple plausible future outcomes. Using AI to scan the horizon, process data, look for patterns, and get a deeper understanding of risks are all examples of where AI can augment the human processes involved in scenario planning.

- AI is having the greatest impact where it enhances, rather than replaces, human activity. Collective intelligence is where AI and humans come together with complementary skills. AI cannot replace humans in the scenario planning process, but it can help with the heavy lifting of data that supports strategic dialogue and complex decision-making.

- When thinking about the deployment of AI in the context of scenario planning, it's important to know the potential business processes where AI can be applied in the end-to-end sequence of activities. But it's equally important to understand the role that broader considerations, relating to leadership, strategy, roles and responsibilities, data, platforms, and governance, play in an organization's success.

CONCLUSION

"The rate of change is not going to slow down anytime soon. If anything, competition in most industries will probably speed up even more in the next few decades."

—JOHN P. KOTTER, HARVARD BUSINESS SCHOOL PROFESSOR

Toward the end of December 2019, the first news of a virus outbreak in China began to appear in the mainstream media and on social media feeds. But it wasn't new. The virus had been present in Wuhan, China, for at least a matter of weeks, if not months. Meanwhile, in Canada, the Public Health Agency of Canada was caught off-guard, which was surprising given Canada had established a team of top doctors and epidemiologists and a state-of-the-art monitoring system scanning the world for early warning signs of significant health threats.

The Global Public Health Intelligence Network (GPHIN) was intended to alert federal officials in Canada, as well as public officials around the world, including the World Health Organization (WHO), to potential threats. It had worked effectively in the past. GPHIN had spotted the earliest signs of H1N1 (2009), MERS (2012), and the largest Ebola outbreak (2014), allowing officials around the world to develop responses.

However, eight months before COVID-19 began to spread, the Public Health Agency of Canada ended the international aspect of GPHIN, deciding the funding was better spent focused on domestic issues, according to an investigation by the *Globe and Mail*.[1] So by January 2020, as signs that the world faced the most explosive and widespread pandemic in a century surfaced, Canada, which would have been on top of the crisis, was unprepared. Even more surprising, GPHIN was still operating internationally in the background and had flagged a pneumonia-like virus in Wuhan in late December 2019. But the medical and scientific staff members, who by then required formal permission to even notify their government bosses of an international report, said their warnings were either ignored, misunderstood, or half-heartedly addressed.

What could have been done had GPHIN's results been taken seriously? Experts could have decided before the pandemic had spread whether to stock up on PPEs and ventilators, set up quarantine centres, begin testing at airports or even shut down incoming flights, prepare hospitals for a potential crisis, or close borders.

What GPHIN was doing didn't precisely conform to scenario planning as I've been describing it in this book. But it precisely mirrors it in the setting-up stage, when plausible scenarios are developed and leaders, forewarned about unforeseen challenges, are able to respond to these potential *what-ifs* and establish an early-warning system that tracks and monitors the threats and risks as part of a process of continuously exploring the external environment. This allows organizations to validate and stress-test the strategies to be sure all eventualities have been considered. For example, as I wrote in Chapter 1, for businesses: "*What if* government introduces new regulations that constrain your organization? *What if* a global conflict disrupts your supply flow? *What if* a disruptor emerges in your sector and shakes up the status quo?"

Or, if you are a government or a business or a non-profit organization or just about any institution, *what if* a massive coronavirus pandemic is about to profoundly disrupt not just your country but the entire world?

GPHIN also conformed to the scenario planning model by using the best tools available—today that includes big data and AI, as I outlined in Chapter 7. Every day, GPHIN analyzed more than 20,000 online news reports (approximately 30,000 sources) in nine languages around the world. A web-based program aggregated the data based on an algorithm that highlighted signals of emerging public health issues, and this information was returned to GPHIN's multilingual and multidisciplinary team. (A good example of AI and humans working together in a collective and intelligent way.) Various examples of AI are involved in the filtering and collecting of relevant data. Today the system has expanded to include data generated by smartphones and social media (such as Twitter and Facebook).[2]

So, although GPHIN wasn't called scenario planning by the federal government, it was set up very much like one and could have provided valuable input into a properly considered scenario planning process. And, just as in businesses, the usefulness of the system is only as good as the organization's willingness to support it.

■ ■ ■

As we reflect over the last 50 years of business and society, it's clear that change is constant, and leaders and organizations are dealing with myriad challenges—many of them new—in this evolving world. Periods of relative calm and stability are inevitably interrupted by periods of massive shocks and disruption that seem to occur whenever they are least expected. These shocks send reverberations through all aspects of how work gets done, and a period of recovery tends to follow. We have experienced one of these moments recently with COVID-19, but as you look back at history's other "shocks," they can be observed in a recurring pattern of every decade or so. There is no reason to suspect this pattern will change, so we should anticipate and prepare for what is coming, because being prepared and resilient are critical to longevity and sustainability in an organization's performance. The only real questions are *When will the next crisis occur?* and *How much of an impact will it have?*

This final chapter provides a brief overview of some of the major market events that have created enormous uncertainty and complexity over the last 50 years, the lessons learned that we should consider, and some final concluding comments and reflections that bring together the various aspects of the preceding chapters.

A HISTORY OF MAJOR GLOBAL EVENTS

So what have been the major global events that have caused economic crisis and considerable market shocks over the last 50 years? What have been the impacts? How frequently do they occur? What should we expect next? These are some of the questions that leaders should be asking themselves as they look to the past for clues about what to expect in the future. Highlighted below are just some of the major catastrophic global events in the last 50 years with a brief assessment of the impacts.

- **The OPEC Oil Price Shock of 1973:** OPEC, which stands for Organization of the Petroleum Exporting Countries, primarily consists of Arab countries, dominated by Saudi Arabia, operating as a cartel controlling 75 percent of the world's crude oil reserves and 42 percent of crude oil output; it therefore typically influences prices traded as Brent Crude and West Texas Intermediate (WTI). In 1973 OPEC retaliated against the United States in response to America's supplying of arms to Israel during the fourth Arab-Israeli war. When OPEC cut oil supplies to the United States and other Western allies, it caused major disruptions and a huge spike in global oil prices, in turn triggering an economic crisis in the United States and other developed countries around the world.

It was interesting to observe during this period that inflation rates were very high, caused in part by the high crude prices and a slowdown in global economic growth, with many economists calling these events a period of "stagflation." It took several years for inflation to fall to normal levels and output to recover. What's also curious about OPEC is how a small group of state-run companies had such immense control over oil supply and could, to their benefit, affect global prices outside free market economies. Organizations operating outside the system in non-OPEC economies have no control over the result.

- **Latin American Sovereign Debt Crisis of 1982:** After a period of exploiting cheap foreign debt for many years, several Latin American countries suddenly realized they were unable to repay that debt. The countries most affected were Argentina, Brazil, and Mexico, which, at the time, had strong and growing economies; banks were content to continue to lend them money, but when the global economy went into recession, interest rates on bond payments rose, currencies crashed, and leaders announced their countries were insolvent.

The region fell into a period of slow growth and recession. The recovery from the crisis took years to achieve, with various IMF bailouts, austerity measures, and market reforms. Lessons learned went unheeded, and years later other parts of the world, including Asia and the Eurozone, experienced the same situation: periods of high borrowing followed by an inability to repay the debts.

- **Tequila Crisis of 1994:** In one week in 1994, the Mexican peso crashed suddenly by nearly 50 percent, followed by a huge interest rate crash, the result appropriately called "The Tequila Crisis." The economic meltdown is believed to have been caused by the new president, Ernesto Zedillo, who devalued the Mexican peso, a shift away from the currency controls of his predecessor. The U.S. government eventually stepped in with a $50 billion bailout in loan guarantees, which caused yields on Mexican debt to increase to 11 percent.[3]

  After a period of instability and uncertainty, the Mexican peso finally stabilized, and the country returned to economic growth. Over the long term, Mexico was able to repay the U.S. loans, and confidence in the country's economy returned.

- **Dot-com Bubble of 2000:** The features of the dot-com crisis of 2000 are well understood today: an overinflated stock market characterized by excessive speculation on Internet and tech-related stocks that were experiencing a period of tremendous growth around the world. Companies with trendy ideas that had yet to produce a finished product, let alone revenues or profits, went to market with initial public offerings and saw their stock prices triple or even quadruple in a day, creating a frenzy for investors. Venture capital investments were hot at the time, and by 1999, 39 percent of all investments were going into tech stocks, with 295 of the 457 IPOs that year being tech-related companies. The Nasdaq market index rose by 400 percent between 1995 and March 2000, before crashing in October of that year—with many online companies going under. Among the few exceptions that weathered the storm were Amazon, Cisco, Intel, and Oracle, all of whom went on to become powerful organizations.[4]

The bubble properly burst from 2001 to 2002, with even many blue-chip companies suffering major losses.

- **Economic Crisis of 2008:** This was also known as the global financial crisis of 2007–08 and was primarily caused by U.S. banks taking excessive risks, the vulnerability of the subprime lending market, and the bankruptcy of Lehman Brothers. The recession that followed was seen by many at the time as the worst global recession since the Great Depression. When the U.S. stock market crashed, it lost almost $8 trillion in value by 2009, unemployment skyrocketed (reaching as high as 10 percent), and Americans lost vast sums of personal wealth in the value of their homes and retirement funds, estimated at $9.8 trillion.[5]

  In its wake, global economic growth dropped by 4 percent. A debt crisis occurred in the European Union, and Greece experienced a near-catastrophic deficit. In order to stabilize global economies and bring reassurance back to the system, governments around the world were forced to bail out banks and other organizations as well as stimulate economies with periods of government spending and stimulus. New regulations, such as the Dodd-Frank Wall Street Reform and Consumer Protection Act in the United States, were introduced to reform the banking systems, so some lessons were learned and applied.

- **COVID-19 Pandemic of 2020:** Between late February and mid-March 2020, global stock markets began to crash, with the largest single week loss since the financial crisis of 2008 and falls of several percentage points on many indices. The full extent of this latest crisis is still unknown as of this writing, as various factors continue to play out in real time and companies react to protect their investments and adapt to the volatile situation. According to the World Health Organization, COVID-19 has now spread to 223 countries, all U.S. states, and as of the time of writing has killed approximately 2.4 million people globally with many more deaths expected in the future.[6] Global economic trade is expected to fall by between 13 and 32 percent, depending on the depth of the economic downturn in various countries, areas, and territories, and the World Bank predicts a 5.2 percent contraction in global GDP in 2020.[7]

Governments have already earmarked trillions in funds to stabilize economies, stimulate growth, and help slow market free fall. Some of the measures seem to be working, but as the crisis drags on, questions are being asked as to what's next and how best to allocate the funds to enable stability and eventual recovery. McKinsey estimates that government deficits could reach $30 trillion by 2023, requiring government and the private sector to work together to prevent the disastrous consequences of huge deficits.[8]

As we begin to understand the full extent of the impact of the pandemic, it's clear that it has damaged many aspects of our lives, both at work and at home. We see impacts on supply-side manufacturing; shortages in essential items; travel restrictions affecting global aviation, transportation, and international tourism; sports and entertainment mostly on hold; bricks-and-mortar retail outlets affected by consumers buying less and moving more and more frequently online; and there's more. There have been shortages of important PPE supplies as well as pharmaceuticals. We've also seen panic buying of vital supplies, leaving shortages of some products in supermarkets, as well as examples of price-gouging. The pub and restaurant trade has imploded. The pandemic has caused the largest global recession in history with more than one-third of the world's population in lockdown at home. Clem Sunter, renowned strategist and scenario planner, indicates four potential scenarios post COVID-19 and believes the world is in the grips of a crisis that looks to be much worse in practical terms than the Great Depression. He believes that life will never return to what it was before the virus started in the Wuhan province in China.[9]

As you reflect on these various crises over the last 50 years, you cannot ignore the possibility that history does repeat itself—we seem to enter into one kind of crisis or another approximately every decade. There is something about the way markets and the wider system operates that seems to result in this cycle of "boom-followed-by-bust," creating the challenge for organizations to predict and prepare for this uncertainty and complexity. The boom has periods of investment, growth, employment, consumption, and excess, followed by the bust period that features austerity, unemployment, investment cuts, bailouts, and new regulations that attempt—but consistently fail—to prevent it from happening again.

According to Rita Gunther McGrath, at Columbia University's business school, and Ian MacMillan, at the Wharton School, after every recession, the world emerges differently from the old one. These researchers believe a discovery-driven approach can help leaders redirect their companies and begin to shape the world that will emerge when the current crisis passes. This is the time, they boldly argue, to disengage from business as usual—including old initiatives, people, and other resources that are weak or under pressure and likely to underperform in the future. It is the time to reconfigure the core, redeploying resources away from the old into new opportunities for growth. Scenario planning offers some of these tools to rethink what that reconfiguration could look like in anticipation of the next major crisis.[10]

Some important questions need to be asked. What have we learned? How can we avoid plunging into crisis again? What could be done differently next time? Can we plan to be ready as an organization for possible futures, no matter how bad and unpredictable they may be? This is not solved just at the company level, but at the political, system, industry, country, and global level. We need better long-term approaches to protect our economies with more sophisticated systems thinking and intelligent organizations. We also need strong leaders who think in diverging directions, involving a variety of approaches, some of which will lead to new, effective ideas (this is the definition of creativity), leaders who factor in the broader external forces and prepare for constant change ahead.

LESSONS LEARNED

As we think about these periods of change and the boom-bust cycles, there are important lessons to be learned that, if factored into the strategic approach of governments, sectors, and organizations, will help build resiliency and limit the impacts when they inevitably come. Outlined below are ten of these lessons that could help lessen future shocks and should influence internal systems, leadership approaches, and systemic behaviours within organizations.

1. **REFLECT on, and avoid, mistakes of the past.** Companies need to resist the urge to expect that there will be a constantly strong and growing economic system and be prepared for the eventual bust cycle that will come. It's sometimes easy to fall into a false sense of reality that things are good and will continue to be good, but history shows time and time again that is not the case. Learn from previous mistakes by reflecting on, and discussing with colleagues, those mistakes and agree on what will be done

differently when the next disruption is upon us. Scenario planning helps leaders reflect on the organization's strategy and evaluate the past, current, and future opportunities.

2. **INVEST in culture and talent as a differentiator.** Proactive investment in organizational culture and the skills and capabilities of a talent base is strongly associated with companies that thrive in challenging conditions, preparing them to take advantage of future upturns. Aspects of this book have addressed the ability to think critically, stretching mental models and including a diversity of perspectives. Scenario planning requires investing in the right skills and talent to prepare for the tough realities ahead.

3. **PREPARE to operate in a tumultuous world.** Stability is a thing of the past in an increasingly uncertain world. Organizations should work toward a better understanding of the changing realities of the market. They can do this by increasing their external understanding and building strategic foresight capabilities. It can be easy to think that things will return to normal, that the next crisis won't be as bad as the last, but history tells us otherwise. A main theme of this book can be summed up as VUCA—Volatility, Uncertainty, Complexity, and Ambiguity. That is what we all face, and scenario planning helps organizations deal with it.

4. **FOCUS on the future, not just the present.** The most resilient companies are those that balance the needs of the present and the future. It's easy to get stuck in the moment, thinking only of the short term, but success is achieved by mixing the short term with a long-term view and ensuring strategies and tactics reflect this balanced approach to strategic thinking. Scenario planning is, of course, a way of preparing to deal with future realities, whatever they may be.

5. **BUILD organizational shock absorbers.** Organizations need to be able to absorb those moments when business is tough, which is something the U.S. banks did not do during the 2007–08 financial crisis. Scenario planning helps leaders ensure their business is stress-tested and resilient. Tools include a strong balance sheet, access to debt financing, a diversified portfolio, and a mix of products and customers.

6. **CONNECT to the external world.** It's important for companies to remain connected to external threats, opportunities, stakeholders, and emerging technologies at all times. The moment an organization's leaders lose sight of this, as shown in the GPHIN example, is the moment they will miss something important that could affect their business. Scenario planning is an important defence, a way to monitor the risks, trends, and uncertainties and assess what they mean to your organization.

7. **LEARN on a continuous basis.** An organization's ability to learn and adapt is an important aspect of overcoming challenges. With the help of scenario planning, leaders can build a business operating model that fosters continual learning—specifically, a deep curiosity to understand changes in their industry, emerging technology, and talent management.

8. **EXPLOIT business opportunities.** Even in the periods of bust it's important to explore and exploit opportunities. Organizations should do so through the pursuit of innovation, which requires leaders to draw on creativity and fearlessness when they recognize fruitful circumstances. Developing this skill will set organizations apart from competitors. Scenario planning helps leaders recognize unnoticed possibilities.

9. **Stay HUMBLE and don't think you're too big to fail.** The global banks thought they were too big to fail, but many of them did (ABN AMRO, Lehman Brothers, and Merrill Lynch, for example), and others would have collapsed without government bailouts. It's important not to become complacent, thinking that size means you are immune to failure. Scenario planning shows you worst-case scenarios, which helps you remain focused, humble, and prepared. Big or small, businesses that understand this will ensure sustainability.

10. **Remember it starts with YOU, not others.** It's easy during a period of crisis to blame others—a broken system, an ineffective government—but the reality is, you only have yourself to blame for not being ready for the crises. It's important to focus on preparing the strategies that will ensure the long-term success of your organization.

THE FUTURE ROLE OF SCENARIO PLANNING

Scenario planning is not something new. As you know, it has been used since the middle of the last century for military planning, followed by its innovative use by Shell, Anglo-American, and other pioneering firms that took it to a new level at the boardroom table. History has shown that as businesses evolve, the management tools, such as scenario planning, evolve with them.

This book has highlighted the importance of investigating the future. Understanding what could happen allows organizations to be better prepared and supports a more sustainable competitive advantage. It's not about forecasting the future, but considering multiple future potential realities and becoming strategically flexible, nimble, innovative, and mentally prepared to deal with whatever the future brings.

There are many benefits to scenario planning, as illustrated in the benefits model, and these depend on the context of the company. Some will be more important and useful than others. Despite this, surprisingly few companies properly leverage scenario planning, but with the massive complexity and uncertainty of COVID-19 unfolding in front of us, the argument for adopting scenario planning has never been more obvious or more urgent.

Modern tools like AI will accelerate the development of new processing powers to handle increasing volumes of data across a number of different business areas. Staying on top of this new thinking and these new technologies through the various end-to-end components of the scenario planning process will be important. Whether it's for competitive insights or external news and social media analysis, the power and capability of AI is constantly growing, and the winners will be those who quickly adopt and adapt to the new technology.

Success is also about scenario planning's ability to help an organization develop shock absorbers to help deal with the next bust, while at the same time preparing for the next boom. Thinking through the options, both good and bad, and tailoring strategies to fit the different eventual realities will make the difference between average- and high-performance organizations. Scenario planning is about seeing around the corner and understanding what could happen next.

We can also open our minds to history and by using scenario planning we can reflect, learn, prepare, focus, seek the best opportunities, wisely invest, build the right portfolio and organizational capabilities, stay humble, and avoid complacency.

In conclusion, scenario planning is about being prepared, resilient, open, innovative, creative, curious, and ready for change. It's about challenging an organization's comfort level and assumptions, stretching mental models, expanding the boundaries of existing strategies, and considering new options however crazy. It's about enabling better collaboration between, and within, organizations.

The future is both daunting and exciting. While we can never predict exactly what will happen and will always be surprised by the unexpected, scenario planning represents an approach that will help us plan and prepare. It is worth the investment of time, talent, and treasury.

NOTES

INTRODUCTION

1. S. Brannen and K. Hicks (2020). "We Predicted a Coronavirus Pandemic. Here's What Policymakers Could Have Seen Coming." *Politico*, March 7, 2020. www.politico.com/news/magazine/2020/03/07/coronavirus-epidemic-prediction-policy-advice-121172.

2. Brannen and Hicks (2020). "We Predicted a Coronavirus Pandemic."

CHAPTER 1

1. Event 201 (2020). "About the Event 201 Exercise." www.centerfor-healthsecurity.org/event201/about

2. R. Bradfield et al. (2005). "The Origins and Evolution of Scenario Techniques in Long Range Business Planning." *Futures* 37(8): 795–812.

3. Shell Scenarios. www.shell.com/energy-and-innovation/the-energy-future/scenarios.html.

4. A. Lakein (1973). *How to Get Control of Your Time and Your Life*. New American Library, 92.

5. G. Burt and K. van der Heijden (2003). "First Steps: Towards Purposeful Activities in Scenario Thinking and Future Studies." *Futures* 35(10): 1011–26.

6. D. Rigby and B. Bilodeau (2018). "Management Tools and Trends." Bain & Company. www.bain.com/insights/management-tools-and-trends-2017/.

7. Gartner (March 2020). "Case Study: How PepsiCo Identifies the Right KPIs." www.gartner.com/en/documents/3982686/case-study-how-pepsico-identifies-the-right-kpis.

8. Author communication and interviews with Manitoba Hydro, 2020.

9. T. J. Chermack (2005). "Studying Scenario Planning: Theory, Research Suggestions, and Hypotheses." *Technological Forecasting and Social Change* 72(1): 59–73.

10. K. van der Heijden (2000). "Scenarios and Forecasting: Two Perspectives." *Technological Forecasting and Social Change* 65(1): 31–36.

11. W. R. Huss and E. J. Honton (1987). "Scenario Planning—What Style Should You Use?" *Long Range Planning* 20(4): 21–29.

12. Burt and van der Heijden (2003). "First Steps."

13. C. A. Varum and C. Melo (2010). "Directions in Scenario Planning Literature—A Review of the Past Decades." *Futures* 42(4): 355–69.

14. J. A. Pearce et al. (1987). "The Tenuous Link Between Formal Strategic Planning and Financial Performance." *Academy of Management Review* 12(4): 658–75.

15. R. Phelps et al. (2001). "Does Scenario Planning Affect Performance? Two Exploratory Studies." *Journal of Business Research* 51(3): 223–32.

16. P. J. Schoemaker (1995). "Scenario Planning: A Tool for Strategic Thinking." *MIT Sloan Management Review* 36(2): 25–50.

CHAPTER 2

1. G. W. Schuurman, A. Symstad, B. W. Miller, A. N. Runyon, and R. Ohms (2019). *Climate Change Scenario Planning for Resource Stewardship: Applying a Novel Approach in Devils Tower National Monument.* Natural Resources Report: National Park Service U.S. Department of Interior. http://irma.nps.gov/DataStore/DownloadFile/.

2. E. Klerk, R. Kersley, M. Bhatti, and B. Vair (August 24, 2017). *Global Equity Themes: Disruptive Forces in Europe: A Primer*. Credit Suisse Equity Research. http://research-doc.credit-suisse.com/docView?language=ENG&format=PDF&sourceid=emgpm&document_id=1079753961&serialid=0FaMPipwKOHKsuTLB1cQRgRSiglHZgp%2BOjvoGfz%2BH1Y%3D&cspId=6666504258438021120&toolbar=1.

3. PhRMA (2015). Biopharmaceutical Research and Development: The Process Behind New Medicines. The Pharmaceutical Research and Manufacturers of America. http://phrma-docs.phrma.org/sites/default/files/pdf/rd_brochure_022307.pdf.

4. U.S. Bureau of Transportation Statistics (July 14, 2020). "Air Traffic Data, May 2020: 89% Reduction in U.S. Airline Passengers from May 2019." www.bts.gov/newsroom/air-traffic-data-may-2020-89-reduction-us-airline-passengers-may-2019-preliminary.

5. Accreditation Council for Graduate Medical Education (2020). *Annual Report*. http://acgme.org/About-Us/Overview/Annual-Report.

6. ACGME (2020). Accreditation Council for Graduate Medical Education—ACGME 2014 Strategic Plan Summary. www.acgme.org/Portals/0/PFAssets/PublicationsPapers/Strategic%20Plan%20Summary.pdf?ver=2015-11-06-120707-670.

7. Accreditation Council for Graduate Medical Education. "2019–2020 Annual Report." https://acgme.org/About-Us/Overview/Annual-Report; T. Nasca and C.W. Thomas (2015). "Medicine in 2035: Selected Insights from ACGME's Scenario Planning," *Journal of Graduate Medical Education* 7(1): 139–142. https://doi.org/10.4300/JGME-D-14-00740.1; ACGME (2020). "Accreditation Council for Graduate Medical Education 2020 Strategic Plan Summary 2020." www.acgme.org/Portals/0/PFAssets/PublicationsPapers/Strategic%20Plan%20Summary.pdf?ver=2015-11-06-120707-670.

8. World Economic Forum (2020). "Justin Trudeau's Davos Address in Full." www.weforum.org/agenda/2018/01/pm-keynote-remarks-for-world-economic-forum-2018/.

9. Tyler Clifford (July 18, 2019). "Bank of America CEO on the Importance of Digital Banking: 'The Numbers Are Just Rolling.'" www.cnbc.com/2019/07/18/bank-of-america-ceo-on-digital-banking-the-numbers-are-just-rolling.html.

10. Adrienne Matei (August 21, 2019). "Shock! Horror! Do You Know How Much Time You Spend on Your Phone?" *Guardian*. www.theguardian. com/lifeandstyle/2019/aug/21/cellphone-screen-time-average-habits#:~:- text=According%20to%20research%20from%20RescueTime,four%20 and%20a%20half%20hours.

11. S. Patel (2019). "Six Forces Disrupting the Power Sector." *Power Magazine*. www.powermag.com/six-forces-disrupting-the-power-sector/.

12. United Nations Department of Economic and Social Affairs (2019). "Growing at a Slower Pace, World Population Is Expected to Reach 9.7 Billion in 2050 and Could Peak at Nearly 11 Billion Around 2100." www. un.org/development/desa/en/news/population/world-population-pros- pects-2019.html.

13. United Nations Data Booklet (2016). "The World's Cities in 2016." www. un.org/en/development/desa/population/publications/pdf/urbanization/ the_worlds_cities_in_2016_data_booklet.pdf.

14. G. Nargund (2009). "Declining Birth Rate in Developed Countries: A Radical Policy Re-think is Required." www.ncbi.nlm.nih.gov/pmc/arti- cles/PMC4255510/.

15. OECD Policy Responses to Coronavirus (COVID-19) (April 23, 2030). "Tracking and Tracing COVID: Protecting Privacy and Data While Using Apps and Biometrics." www.oecd.org/coronavirus/policy-responses/ tracking-and-tracing-covid-protecting-privacy-and-data-while-using- apps-and-biometrics-8f394636/.

16. Emily Dayton (n.d.). "Amazon Statistics You Should Know: Opportunities to Make the Most of America's Top Online Marketplace." BigCommerce. com. www.bigcommerce.com/blog/amazon-statistics/#:~:text=In%20 2018%2C%20Amazon's%20share%20of,%25%20and%20Walmart%20 at%203.7%25.

17. Philip Walsh (2005). "Dealing with the Uncertainties of Environmen- tal Change by Adding Scenario Planning to the Strategy Reformulation Equation." *Management Decision* 43(1): 113–22.

18. The Associated Press (2020). "Zoom Profits Soar as Pandemic Spurs Boom in Video Chatting." www.cbc.ca/news/business/zoom-earnings-1.5596289.

19. J. J. Oliver and E. Parrett (2018). "Managing Future Uncertainty: Reeval- uating the Role of Scenario Planning." *Business Horizons* 61(2): 339–52.

20. E. Bonabeau (2007). "Understanding and Managing Complexity Risk." *MIT Sloan Management Review* 48(4): 62.

21. J. Desjardins (2019). "How Much Data Is Generated Each Day?" World Economic Forum. www.weforum.org/agenda/2019/04/how-much-data-is-generated-each-day-cf4bddf29f/.

22. R. Ramírez et al. (June 13, 2017)."Using Scenario Planning to Reshape Strategy," *MIT Sloan Management Review*. https://sloanreview.mit.edu/article/using-scenario-planning-to-reshape-strategy/.

23. Bonabeau (2007). "Understanding and Managing Complexity Risk."

24. Tim Cooper (August 12, 2020). "Covid-19 Recovery Pushes CFOs to Improve Scenario Planning." *Financial Management*. www.fm-magazine.com/news/2020/aug/coronavirus-recovery-pushes-cfos-to-improve-scenario-planning.html.

25. D. Carlucci et al. (2010). "Managing Complexity: Systems Thinking as a Catalyst of the Organization Performance." *Measuring Business Excellence* 14(4): 49–64.

26. L. R. Jauch and K. L. Kraft (1986). "Strategic Management of Uncertainty." *Academy of Management Review* 11(4): 777–90.

27. M. Schwaninger (2000). "Managing Complexity—The Path Toward Intelligent Organizations." *Systemic Practice and Action Research* 13(2): 207–41.

28. D. Van Beek (2015). "The Contours of the Intelligent Organization." Passionned Group. www.passionned.com/the-contours-of-the-intelligent-organization/.

29. R. Vecchiato (2019). "Scenario Planning, Cognition, and Strategic Investment Decisions in a Turbulent Environment." *Long Range Planning* 52(5): 101865.

30. G. Burt and K. van der Heijden (2003). "First Steps: Towards Purposeful Activities in Scenario Thinking and Future Studies." *Futures* 35(10): 1011–26.

31. A. Sörman-Nilsson (2020). "Re-Emergence: The 2nd Renaissance of Human Creativity." www.anderssorman-nilsson.com/blog/re-emergence-the-2nd-renaissance-of-human-creativity.

CHAPTER 3

1. K. Moyer (1996). "Scenario Planning at British Airways—A Case Study." *Long Range Planning* 29(2): 172–81. www.sciencedirect.com/science/article/abs/pii/0024630196000052.

2. P. J. Schoemaker (1995). "Scenario Planning: A Tool for Strategic Thinking." *MIT Sloan Management Review* 36(2): 25–50. http://sloanreview.mit.edu/article/scenario-planning-a-tool-for-strategic-thinking/.

3. P. Cornelius et al. (2005). "Three Decades of Scenario Planning in Shell." *California Management Review* 48(1): 92–109. http://strategy.sjsu.edu/www.stable/B290/reading/Cornelius,%20P.,%20A.%20Van%20de%20Putte,%20et%20al.,%202005,%20California%20Management%20Review%2048(1)%2092-109.pdf.

4. A. Cann (2010). "Scenario-Based Strategic Planning in the U.S. Army Corps of Engineers Civil Works Program." Institute for Water Resources. www.iwr.usace.army.mil/Portals/70/docs/iwrreports/Scenario-BasedStrategicPlanning.pdf.

5. IWR White Paper (June 2010). "Scenario-Based Strategic Planning in the U.S. Army Corps of Engineers Civil Works Program." www.iwr.usace.army.mil/Portals/70/docs/iwrreports/Scenario-BasedStrategicPlanning.pdf.

6. A. Kleiner (1996). "Virtual Consulting New York: Shell's Scenario Planning 1998." http://royaldutchshellplc.com/1996/01/06/virtual-consulting-new-york-shells-scenario-planning-1998/.

7. Business-to-You (2016). "Scanning the Environment: PESTEL Analysis." www.business-to-you.com/scanning-the-environment-pestel-analysis/.

8. Michael E. Porter (1979). "How Competitive Forces Shape Strategy." *Harvard Business Review* 57(2): 137–45.

9. J. Pongthanaisawan et al. (2018). "Scenario Planning for Low Carbon Tourism City: A Case Study of Nan." *Energy Procedia* 152: 715–24. www.sciencedirect.com/science/article/pii/S187661021830780X.

10. Robert S. Kaplan and David P. Norton (1992). "The Balanced Scorecard—Measures that Drive Performance." *Harvard Business Review* (January–February 1992).

11. A "leading" indicator looks at outcomes and events in the future. A "lagging" indicator looks back to see whether an intended result was achieved.

CHAPTER 4

1. Adam Kahane (2012). *Working Together to Change the Future: Transformative Scenario Planning*. Berrett-Koehler Publishers, Inc., 1–6.

2. A. Kahane (n.d). "The Mont Fleur Scenarios: What Will South Africa Be Like in the Year 2002?" *Deeper News* 7(1). https://reospartners.com/wp-content/uploads/old/Mont%20Fleur.pdf.

3. P. Cornelius et al. (2005). "Three Decades of Scenario Planning in Shell." *California Management Review* 48(1): 92–109.

4. J. Verity (2003). "Scenario Planning as a Strategy." *European Business Journal* 5(4): 185–95.

5. R. F. Korte (2008). "Applying Scenario Planning Across Multiple Levels of Analysis." *Advances in Developing Human Resources* 10(2): 179–97.

6. H. Courtney (2003). "Decision-Driven Scenarios for Assessing Four Levels of Uncertainty." *Strategy & Leadership* 31(1):14–22.

7. R. J. Epstein (May 24, 2020; updated July 18, 2020). "Trump Sows Doubt on Voting. It Keeps Some People Up at Night." *New York Times*. www.nytimes.com/2020/05/24/us/politics/trump-2020-election-voting-rights.html?smid=em-share.

8. E. F. Schumacher (1978). *A Guide for the Perplexed*. Harper Perennial.

9. K. Leung et al. (2020). "First-Wave COVID-19 Transmissibility and Severity in China Outside Hubei After Control Measures, and Second-Wave Scenario Planning: A Modelling Impact Assessment." *The Lancet* 395(10233): 1382–93.

10. Centers for Disease Control and Prevention (2020). "COVID-19 Pandemic Planning Scenarios." www.cdc.gov/coronavirus/2019-ncov/hcp/planning-scenarios.html.

11. M.-S. Chang et al. (2007). "A Scenario Planning Approach for the Flood Emergency Logistics Preparation Problem Under Uncertainty." *Transportation Research Part E: Logistics and Transportation Review* 43(6): 737–54.

12. G. D. Peterson et al. (2003). "Scenario Planning: A Tool for Conservation in an Uncertain World." *Conservation Biology* 17(2): 358–66.

13. R. Ramírez et al. (June 13, 2017). "Using Scenario Planning to Reshape Strategy," *MIT Sloan Management Review*. https://sloanreview.mit.edu/article/using-scenario-planning-to-reshape-strategy/; Royal Society of

Chemistry (n.d.). "Future of the Chemical Sciences." www.rsc.org/glo-balassets/04-campaigning-outreach/campaigning/future-chemical-sciences/future-of-the-chemical-science-report-royal-society-of-chemistry.pdf; H. Pain (June 1, 2020). "Community Minded." *Chemistry World.* www.chemistryworld.com/opinion/community-minded/4011867.article.

14. Korte (2008). "Applying Scenario Planning Across Multiple Levels of Analysis."

15. J. Allwood et al. (2008). "An Approach to Scenario Analysis of the Sustainability of an Industrial Sector Applied to Clothing and Textiles in the UK." *Journal of Cleaner Production* 16(12): 1234–46.

16. F. Davies et al. (2005). "Constructing a Knowledge-Based System to Aid Scenario-Based Strategic Planning: An Application to the European Airline Industry." *Intelligent Systems in Accounting, Finance & Management: International Journal* 13(2): 61–79.

17. C. Zegras et al. (2004). "Scenario Planning for Strategic Regional Transportation Planning." *Journal of Urban Planning and Development* 130(1): 2–13.

18. Cornelius et al. (2005). "Three Decades of Scenario Planning in Shell."

19. J. M. Lambert and M. J. Schroeder (2009). "Scenario-Based Transportation Planning with Involvement of Metropolitan Planning Organizations." Virginia Transportation Research Council. www.virginiadot.org/vtrc/main/online_reports/pdf/09-cr5.pdf.

20. L. A. Boden et al. (2015). "Scenario Planning: The Future of the Cattle and Sheep Industries in Scotland and Their Resiliency to Disease." *Preventive Veterinary Medicine* 121(3–4): 353–64.

21. International Atomic Energy Agency. www.iaea.org/about.

22. IAEA (International Atomic Energy Agency), "About Us." www.iaea.org; R. Ramírez et al. (January 28, 2020). "Scenario Planning in Science-Centric Organizations." Wiley Online Library. https://doi.org/10.1002/ffo2.30.

23. E. Tapinos (2013). "Scenario Planning at Business Unit Level." *Futures* 47: 17–27.

24. Cornelius et al. (2005). "Three Decades of Scenario Planning in Shell."

25. M. Hussain et al. (2017). "Scenario-Driven Roadmapping for Technology Foresight." *Technological Forecasting and Social Change* (124): 160–177. https://doi.org/10.1016/j.techfore.2017.05.005; GS1 UK. "About Us." www.gs1uk.org/about-us/our-work-with-industry/healthcare-user-group.

26. T. J. Chermack and T. D. Payne (2006). "Process Level Scenario Planning." *Academy of Strategic Management Journal* 5: 115–31.

27. W. R. Huss and E. J. Honton (1987). "Scenario Planning—What Style Should You Use?" *Long Range Planning* 20(4): 21–29.

CHAPTER 5

1. U.S Coast Guard Evergreen Process (2005). "Creating and Sustaining Strategic Intent in the Coast Guard." U.S. Coast Guard.

2. Board of Governors of the Federal Reserve System (2020). "Federal Reserve Board Releases Hypothetical Scenarios for Second Round of Bank Stress Tests." Press release. www.federalreserve.gov/newsevents/pressreleases/bcreg20200917a.htm.

3. P. Wack (1985). "Scenarios: Uncharted Waters Ahead." *Harvard Business Review*. http://hbr.org/1985/09/scenarios-uncharted-waters-ahead.

4. P. Goodwin and G. Wright (2001). "Enhancing Strategy Evaluation in Scenario Planning: A Role for Decision Analysis." *Journal of Management Studies* 38(1): 1–16.

5. P. J. Schoemaker (1991). "When and How to Use Scenario Planning: A Heuristic Approach with Illustration." *Journal of Forecasting* 10(6): 549–64.

6. A. Wright (2000). "Scenario Planning: A Continuous Improvement Approach to Strategy." *Total Quality Management* 11(4–6): 433–38.

7. Monitor Deloitte (March 24, 2015). "Port 2050 Scenarios Update: Final Report." www.portvancouver.com/wp-content/uploads/2015/03/2015-04-07-Port-2050-Scenario-Refresh-Final-Report-with-appendices.pdf; Port of Vancouver. "Port 2050." www.portvancouver.com/about-us/sustainability/port-2050/; G. Feller (October 29, 2019). "Port Authority Leads Energy Transition at the Port of Vancouver," T&D World. www.tdworld.com/distributed-energy-resources/demand-side-management/article/20973318/port-authority-leads-energy-transition-at-the-port-of-vancouver.

8. B. Fagan (2018). "Lessons from Fedex's Zapmail Service." Medium.com. http://medium.com/@bridgetfagan3/a-lesson-in-failure-zapmail-45a90c-b3793e.

9. Eric Bonabeau (May 2003). "Don't Trust Your Gut." *Harvard Business Review*. http://hbr.org/2003/05/dont-trust-your-gut.

10. T. J. Chermack (2004). "Improving Decision-Making with Scenario Planning." *Futures* 36(3): 295–309.

11. T. J. Chermack (2005). "Studying Scenario Planning: Theory, Research Suggestions, and Hypotheses." *Technological Forecasting and Social Change* 72(1): 59–73.

12. K. M. Eisenhardt (1989). "Making Fast Strategic Decisions in High-Velocity Environments." *Academy of Management Journal* 3: 543–76.

13. D. A. Garvin et al. (March 2008). "Is Yours a Learning Organization?" *Harvard Business Review*. www.alnap.org/system/files/content/resource/files/main/r0803h-pdf-eng.pdf.

14. T. J. Chermack et al. (2006). "Exploring the Relationship Between Scenario Planning and Perceptions of Learning Organization Characteristics." *Futures* 38(7): 767–77.

15. K. van der Heijden (2004). "Can Internally Generated Futures Accelerate Organizational Learning?" *Futures* 36(2): 145–59.

16. European Patent Office. "About Us." www.epo.org/about-us.html; R. Ramírez et al. (January 28, 2020). "Scenario Planning in Science-Centric Organizations," Wiley Online Library. https://doi.org/10.1002/ffo2.30.

17. A. Hartung (2008). "Scenario Planning at Apple." http://adamhartung.com/scenario-planning-at-apple/.

18. J. Dyer et al. (2014). "The Industries Plagued by the Most Uncertainty." *Harvard Business Review*. http://hbr.org/2014/09/the-industries-plagued-by-the-most-uncertainty.

19. Philip Walsh (2005). "Dealing with the Uncertainties of Environmental Change by Adding Scenario Planning to the Strategy Reformulation Equation." *Management Decision* 43(1): 113–22.

20. D. Carlucci et al. (2010). "Managing Complexity: Systems Thinking as a Catalyst of the Organization Performance." *Measuring Business Excellence* 14(4): 49–64.

21. A. Rawluk and A. Godber (2011). "Widening the Scope of Scenario Planning in Small Communities: A Case Study Use of an Alternative Method." *Ecology and Society* 16(1). www.jstor.org/stable/26268829.

22. J. McNish and S. Silcoff (May 22, 2015). "The Inside Story of How the iPhone Crippled Blackberry." *The Wall Street Journal*. www.wsj.com/articles/behind-the-rise-and-fall-of-blackberry-1432311912.

23. E. Bonabeau (2007). "Understanding and Managing Complexity Risk." *MIT Sloan Management Review* 48(4): 62.

24. T. M. Alessandri et al. (2004). "Managing Risk and Uncertainty in Complex Capital Projects." *The Quarterly Review of Economics and Finance* 44(5): 751–67.

25. A. Powch (2017). "Overcoming Uncertainty with the Aid of Scenario Planning." *IndustryWeek.* www.industryweek.com/leadership/article/22024354/overcoming-uncertainty-with-the-aid-of-scenario-planning.

26. J. Sueres (2016). "The Future of Newspapers in the Digital Age." Medium.com. http://medium.com/international-online-journalism/the-future-of-newspapers-in-the-digital-age-c7ac8a118312.

27. Schoemaker (1991). "When and How to Use Scenario Planning."

28. Barbara Bilodeau and Darrell K. Rigby (July–August 2007). "A Growing Focus on Preparedness." *Harvard Business Review.* http://hbr.org/2007/07/a-growing-focus-on-preparedness.

29. William J. Worthington, Jamie D. Collins, and Michael A. Hitt (2009). "Beyond Risk Mitigation: Enhancing Corporate Innovation with Scenario Planning." *Business Horizons* 52: 441–50. www.sciencedirect.com/science/article/abs/pii/S0007681309000603.

30. Schoemaker (1991). "When and How to Use Scenario Planning"; Alessandri et al. (2004). "Managing Risk and Uncertainty in Complex Capital Projects"; and Bonabeau (2007). "Understanding and Managing Complexity Risk."

31. S. A. Drew (2006). "Building Technology Foresight: Using Scenarios to Embrace Innovation." *European Journal of Innovation Management* 9(3): 241–57.

32. BMJ Report (2017). "Scenario Planning: Future of Global Research." www.bmj.com/company/scenarioplanning-2/.

33. D. Sarpong and M. Maclean (2011). "Scenario Thinking: A Practice-Based Approach for the Identification of Opportunities for Innovation." *Futures* 43(10): 1154–63.

34. K. Shimizu and M. A. Hitt (2004). "Strategic Flexibility: Organizational Preparedness to Reverse Ineffective Strategic Decisions." *Academy of Management Perspectives* 18(4): 44–59.

35. D. A. Aaker and B. Mascarenhas (1984). "The Need for Strategic Flexibility." *The Journal of Business Strategy* 5(2): 74.

CHAPTER 6

1. M. Fitzgerald (2020). "2019 Had the Most CEO Departures on Record with More than 1,600." CNBC. www.cnbc.com/2020/01/07/2019-had-the-most-ceo-departures-on-record-with-more-than-1600.html.

2. S. Goldstein (2017). "How Tony Hsieh Transformed Zappos with These 5 Core Values." *Inc.* www.inc.com/steve-goldstein/5-ways-zappos-ceo-wins-at-customer-focus-leadership-and-has-for-nearly-20-years.html.

3. M. Schwantes (2017). "The World's 10 Top CEOs (They Lead in a Totally Unique Way)." *Inc.* www.inc.com/marcel-schwantes/heres-a-top-10-list-of-the-worlds-best-ceos-but-they-lead-in-a-totally-unique-wa.html.

4. John P. Kotter (2008). *A Sense of Urgency.* Harvard Business Review Press. Review available: www.leadershipnow.com/leadershop/9781422179710.html.

5. G. Bradt (2018). "How CEOs Best Lead Strategic, Organizational and Operational Processes." *Forbes.* www.forbes.com/sites/george-bradt/2018/04/17/how-ceos-best-lead-strategic-organizational-and-operational-processes/#63e12ba51eae.

6. C. Aiken and S. Keller (2007). "The CEO's Role in Leading Transformation." McKinsey & Company. www.mckinsey.com/business-functions/organization/our-insights/the-ceos-role-in-leading-transformation.

7. BMJ (n.d.). "Our Story." www.bmj.com/company/the-story-of-bmj-2/.

8. S. Rhoods and A. Babor (2018). "The Future of Global Research: A Case Study on the Use of Scenario Planning in the Publishing Industry." Wiley Online Library. http://onlinelibrary.wiley.com/doi/full/10.1002/leap.1152.

9. L. Mortlock (2019). "The DNA of the Chief Strategy Officer." EY. http://assets.ey.com/content/dam/ey-sites/ey-com/en_ca/topics/performance-improvement/ey-dna-of-the-chief-strategy-officer.pdf.

10. T. Schoenwaelder (2019). "The Making of a Successful Chief Strategy Officer." Deloitte Consulting. www2.deloitte.com/us/en/pages/operations/articles/making-of-a-successful-chief-strategy-officer.html.

11. M. Birshan, E. Gibbs, and K. Strovink (2015). "What Makes a Great Chief Strategy Officer." *Harvard Business Review.* http://hbr.org/2015/05/what-makes-a-great-chief-strategy-officer.

12. Brianne Carlon Rush (2014). "Science of Storytelling: Why and How to Use It in Your Marketing." *The Guardian.* www.theguardian.com/media-network/media-network-blog/2014/aug/28/science-storytelling-digital-marketing#:~:text=Our%20brains%20are%20wired%20to,is%20persuasion%20and%20sometimes%20action.%E2%80%9D.

13. P. Nunes (2007). "The Chief Strategy Officer." *Harvard Business Review.* http://ogsp.typepad.com/focus_or_die_ogsp/files/HBR_CSO_October_2007.pdf.

14. N. Kachaner and S. Stewart (2013). "Understanding the Role of the Chief Strategy Officer." The Boston Consulting Group. www.bcg.com/publications/2013/strategic-planning-understanding-role-chief-strategy-officer.aspx.

15. B. de Wit and Ron Meyer (2010). "How Scenario Planning Influences Strategic Decisions," in *Strategy: Process, Content, Context.* Cengage Learning. http://books.google.ca/books?id=tCspQP0CYgcC&pg=PA709&dq=UPS+scenario+planning+mail+boxes+etc&hl=en&sa=X&ved=0ahUKEwiElJudzvrpAhWIIDQIHXQhAzIQ6AEIJzAA#v=onepage&q=UPS%20scenario%20planning%20mail%20boxes%20etc&f=false.

16. Paul J. H. Schoemaker (1995). "Scenario Planning: A Tool for Strategic Thinking." *MIT Sloan Management Review* 36(2): 25–40. www.ftms.edu.my/images/Document/MOD001074%20-%20Strategic%20Management%20Analysis/WK4_SR_MOD001074_Schoemaker_1995.pdf.

CHAPTER 7

1. C. Clifford (March 26, 2019). "Bill Gates: A.I. Is Like Nuclear Energy —'Both Promising and Dangerous'." CNBC. www.cnbc.com/2019/03/26/bill-gates-artificial-intelligence-both-promising-and-dangerous.html#:~:text=%E2%80%9CThe%20world%20hasn't%20had,Intelligence%20Symposium%20at%20Stanford%20University.&text=Jeff%20Bezos%20has%20also%20expressed%20concerns%20about%20killer%20AI.

2. K. Awalegaonkar et al. (2019). "AI: Built to Scale." Accenture.com. www.accenture.com/us-en/insights/artificial-intelligence/ai-investments.

3. D. Baird (December 8, 2017). "NASA Explores Artificial Intelligence for Space Communications." NASA Space Communications. www.nasa.gov/feature/goddard/2017/nasa-explores-artificial-intelligence-for-space-communications.

4. M. Dimitracopoulos, M. Bertolino, and C. David (October 29, 2018). "The Future Workplace: How to Automate Intelligently." EY. www.ey.com/en_ca/workforce/how-do-you-ensure-you-are-automating-intelligently.

5. J.-F. Orsini (1986). "Artificial Intelligence: A Way Through the Strategic Planning Crisis?" *Long Range Planning* 19(4): 71–77.

6. David W. Cearley, Brian Burke, Samantha Searle, and Mike J. Walker (2017). "Top Ten Strategic Technology Trends for 2018." Gartner Inc. www.gartner.com/ngw/globalassets/en/information-technology/documents/top-10-strategic-technology-trends-for-2018.pdf.

7. H. J. Watson (2017). "Preparing for the Cognitive Generation of Decision Support." *MIS Quarterly Executive* 16(3): 153–69.

8. A. DiFranza (November 29, 2019). "The Biggest Data Analytics Challenges of 2020." Northeastern University Graduate Programs. www.northeastern.edu/graduate/blog/data-analytics-challenges/.

9. W. E. Spangler (1991). "The Role of Artificial Intelligence in Understanding the Strategic Decision-Making Process." *IEEE Transactions on Knowledge and Data Engineering* 3(2): 149–59.

10. H. J. Wilson and P. R. Daugherty (2018). "Collaborative Intelligence: Humans and AI Are Joining Forces." *Harvard Business Review* 96(4): 114–23.

11. Yash Raj Shrestha, George von Krough, and Shiko M. Ben-Menahem (July 2019). "Organizational Decision-Making Structures in the Age of AI." *California Management Review* 61(4). www.researchgate.net/publication/334447755_Organizational_Decision-Making_Structures_in_the_Age_of_Artificial_Intelligence.

12. SEB (October 27, 2017). "SEB Awarded for Innovative Use of AI Technology." Press release. http://sebgroup.com/press/news/seb-awarded-for-innovative-use-of-ai-technology.

13. M. H. Jarrahi (2018). "Artificial Intelligence and the Future of Work: Human-AI Symbiosis in Organizational Decision Making." *Business Horizons* 61: 578.

14. R. Hoefnagels et al. (2012). "Capacity Study for Solid Biomass Facilities," for Port of Rotterdam. www.portofrotterdam.com/sites/default/files/PoR-Capacity-study-Scenarios.pdf; Port of Rotterdam (n.d.). "European Hub for Biomass." www.portofrotterdam.com/sites/default/files/european-hup-for-biomass-port-of-rotterdam.pdf?token=hpNVWJXR.

15. T. D. Chowdhury (2019). "Strategic Foresight Development Through AI Based Horizon Scanning." LinkedIn Post. www.linkedin.com/pulse/strategic-foresight-development-through-ai-based-tamal-chowdhury/.

16. P. Wack (September 1985). "Scenarios: Uncharted Waters Ahead," *Harvard Business Review*. https://hbr.org/1985/09/scenarios-uncharted-waters-ahead?registration=success; Shell. "Meet the Shell Scenarios Team." www.shell.com/energy-and-innovation/the-energy-future/scenarios/meet-the-shell-scenarios-team.html.

17. S. Aziz and M. M. Dowling (2018). "AI and Machine Learning for Risk Management." Published as "Machine Learning and AI for Risk Management," in T. Lynn, G. Mooney, P. Rosati, and M. Cummins (eds.) (2019), *Disrupting Finance: FinTech and Strategy in the 21st Century*. Palgrave: 33–50.

18. S. Sohrabi et al. (2018). "An AI Planning Solution to Scenario Generation for Enterprise Risk Management." Thirty-Second AAAI Conference on Artificial Intelligence.

19. A. Tate et al. (2000). "Using AI Planning Technology for Army Small Unit Operations." AIPS 2000 Proceedings. www.aaai.org.

20. A. McGovern et al. (2017). "Using Artificial Intelligence to Improve Real-Time Decision-Making for High-Impact Weather." *Bulletin of the American Meteorological Society* 98(10): 2073–90.

21. H. J. Watson (2017). "Preparing for the Cognitive Generation of Decision Support." *MIS Quarterly Executive* 16(3):153–69. www.researchgate.net/publication/319929429_Preparing_for_the_cognitive_generation_of_decision_support.

22. S. Miller and D. Hughes (2017). "The Quant Crunch: How the Demand for Data Science Skills Is Disrupting the Job Market." Burning Glass Technologies. www.ibm.com/downloads/cas/3RL3VXGA.

23. J. Wallen (May 26, 2019). "Can Outsourcing Data Scientists Fill the Jobs Shortage? Fayrix Believes So." Forbes.com. www.forbes.com/sites/joewalleneurope/2019/03/26/can-outsourcing-data-science-fill-the-jobs-shortage-fayrix-believes-so/#737ebaebce7b.

24. D. Shapiro (2019). "Can Artificial Intelligence Generate Corporate Strategy?" Forbes.com. www.forbes.com/sites/danielshapiro1/2019/08/19/can-artificial-intelligence-generate-corporate-strategy/#75bc2455559f.

25. P. van Kessell (2014). "Big Data: Changing the Way Businesses Compete and Operate." EY. http://pdf4pro.com/view/big-data-changing-the-way-businesses-compete-and-operate-405c89.html.

26. A. Hill (2019). "Artificial Intelligence Creates Real Strategic Dilemmas." FT.com. www.ft.com/content/8e3d9386-77c6-11e9-bbad-7c18c0ea0201.

CONCLUSION

1. Grant Robertson (July 25, 2020). "Without Early Warning You Can't Have Early Response: How Canada's World-Class Pandemic Alert System Failed." *Globe and Mail*. www.theglobeandmail.com/canada/article-with-out-early-warning-you-cant-have-early-response-how-canadas/.

2. M. Dion, Malik Abdel, and A. Mawueku (2015). "Big Data and the Global Public Health Intelligence Network." Government of Canada. www.canada.ca/en/public-health/services/reports-publications/canada-communicable-disease-report-ccdr/monthly-issue/2015-41/ccdr-volume-41-9-september-3-2015-data/ccdr-volume-41-9-september-3-2015-data-1.html.

3. James Chen (July 8, 2020). "The 1994 Mexican Peso Crisis." Investopedia. www.investopedia.com/terms/t/tequilaeffect.asp.

4. Adam Hayes (June 25, 2019). "Dotcom Bubble." Investopedia. www.investopedia.com/terms/d/dotcom-bubble.asp.

5. Renae Merle (September 10, 2018). "A Guide to the Financial Crisis—10 Years Later." *Washington Post*. www.washingtonpost.com/business/economy/a-guide-to-the-financial-crisis--10-years-later/2018/09/10/114b76ba-af10-11e8-a20b-5f4f84429666_story.html.

6. World Health Organization. "Coronavirus Disease (COVID-19) Pandemic." www.who.int/emergencies/diseases/novel-coronavirus-2019.

7. The World Bank. "COVID-19 to Plunge Global Economy into Worst Recession since World War II." Press release. www.worldbank.org/en/news/press-release/2020/06/08/covid-19-to-plunge-global-economy-into-worst-recession-since-world-war-ii.

8. Rima Assi, David Fine, and Kevin Sneader (June 16, 2020). "The Great Balancing Act: Managing the Coming $30 Trillion Deficit While Restoring Economic Growth." www.mckinsey.com/industries/public-and-social-sector/our-insights/the-great-balancing-act-managing-the-coming-30-trillion-dollar-deficit-while-restoring-economic-growth#.

9. J. Cameron (2020). "Clem Sunter: What Life Will Be Like as We Lift Covid-19 Lockdown—Four Scenarios." Biznews. www.biznews.com/inside-covid-19/2020/04/20/covid-19-lockdown-scenarios-clem-sunter.

10. R. G. McGrath and I. C. MacMillan (2009). "How to Rethink Your Business During Uncertainty." *MIT Sloan Management Review.* http://sloanreview.mit.edu/article/how-to-rethink-your-business-during-uncertainty/.

ACKNOWLEDGEMENTS

Analogous to my work as a strategic advisor, this research and writing process has been one of considerable conversation, exploration, and continuous testing of ideas with all kinds of people, including family, friends, colleagues, clients, fellow writers, and academics. Numerous observations, insights, and recommendations have originated from the outside while the book was underway and have been incorporated into the text. I've tried to do my best with the endnotes, but the influences are too numerous to fully capture.

For the various discussions and engagements over the last several years that have helped solidify and sharpen my thinking on strategic processes such as scenario planning, I'm thankful to Jarod Thomson, Annie Murphy, Chris Palmer, Mauricio Zelaya, Jason Rakochy, Samantha Stuart, Rob Palmer, Peter Sherer, Khalid Abdul Razak, Simon Raby, Darren Yaworsky, Mary Moran, Court Ellingson, Bob Sartor, Michael Treacy,

Clem Sunter, Charles Duncan, Paul Selway, Bruno Francoeur, Tristan Goodman, Brent Nadeau, Shaun Kelly, Quinn Wilson, Mitchell White, Michael Lindsey, Mark Becker, Murray Bickley, Mark Chyc-Cies, Tami Kjerulf, Scott Matson, Jaana Woiceshyn, Ben Bazinet, Russ McClung, Rob Morgan, Chris Stuart, Victoria McQueen, Mark Poweska, Kelly Grier, Catherine Mcleod-Seltzer, Sue Paish, Richard Haskayne, Charles-Antoine St-Jean, Jim Dewald, Helen Wesley, Steve Phillips, Mark Little, Peter Zoccali, David Williams, and Kiran Somanchi. My apologies to everybody else who ought to have been remembered here.

For strategic comments on the manuscript highlighting the importance of wider audience appeal, walking me through the book publishing process with patience, and taking my project on, I'm grateful to Sarah Scott.

For detailed comments, pushing the importance of storytelling, bringing the book to life, and helping me prepare the manuscript, I'm extremely grateful to David Hayes.

For ongoing career and life guidance, I'm thankful to my dad, Richard, my mum, Jennie, and mentor Scott Garvey. I'm also thankful to Howard Blight who has always pushed and inspired me to do more.

Finally, a heartfelt thank you to my wife, Elisabeth, and my daughters, Penelope and Olivianne, whose love, unwavering support, and understanding has made all of this possible.

INDEX

ABOUT THE AUTHOR

 **Lance Mortlock** is a senior strategy partner with Ernst & Young, based in Canada. He has provided management consulting services for over 20 years to more than 60 organizations in 11 countries, overseeing hundreds of projects. Mortlock has worked with C-suite executives at leading national and international companies on their most complex strategic problems in mining, oil and gas, power and utility, manufacturing, airline, infrastructure, and government and public sector organizations.

Bringing a broad set of strategic skills and experiences, Lance helps clients solve some of their most complex strategic problems. Areas of expertise and experience include corporate strategy and planning, strategy execution, market opportunity assessment, merger and transaction integration and carve-outs ($60 billion in deals completed), cost management, transformation, innovation, business management systems, process improvement, enterprise risk management, organization performance, design and effectiveness, and change management.

As a strategist, Lance has authored 30 articles on a variety of important business topics. He is also an expert in energy industry trends and market dynamics in Canada, featuring in various industry publications as well as national and international newspapers. He's been on BNN several times, sharing insights on job automation and the transition to electric vehicles.

Lance graduated from Exeter University and earned an MBA from Cardiff Business School, is a Certified Management Consultant, Certified Change Management Professional, Certified Six Sigma Black Belt, and a Project Management Professional. He studied corporate innovation at Stanford Graduate School of Business, artificial intelligence at MIT, and advanced strategy at INSEAD. He is a Visiting Professor at the University of Calgary Haskayne School of Business, and also serves on the Board of the Canadian Energy and Climate Nexus, a non-governmental, non-profit organization to help Canadians develop energy systems in balance with climate change constraints through collaborative problem-solving, collective commitment, and bold action.

Lance is married to Elisabeth, and they have two daughters, Penelope and Olivianne.